Endorsements

No one can read Dr. Gwynn's book without seeing the contrast between the love of God reflected in the Christian faith and the dictatorial hatred of radical Islam. Every student seeking truth must read this book.

-Bill Ligon, Sr.
Pastor Christian Renewal Church – Brunswick, GA
Founder The Father's Blessing

Dr. Gwynn has captured in critical detail the many and great differences between Christianity and Islam, which means "submission." He concludes, "I believe that I have proven that Christianity's efficacy far surpasses Islam's and can be the only true faith a person must believe." Almost all who read this book will agree. Dr. Gwynn graphically demonstrates how Allah is very different from the God of the Bible, and how vastly inferior is Muhammad compared to Jesus. He shows the extremely vast differences in their requirements for salvation and how evangelism is practiced and also how the Christian way of godly love is far superior to the Islamic practice of forced submission. Islam as a religion and as a political system cannot be separated, and the ultimate goal is forcibly to impose Allah's will and shari'ah law on the entire world. Dr. Gwynn has covered far more information than I can describe in this short recommendation. His account of the Crusades and the impossibility of Muhammad being a descendant of Ishmael in the Appendices are very helpful. This is a well-written and documented book and may very likely become a standard text on this subject.

-Rev. James Murk, Ph.D.
Author of the two *Islam Rising* books:
The Never Ending Jihad Against Christianity
The Never Ending Jihad Against The Jews and Israel

This book is rich in facts, insights and understanding. Dr. Gwynn has brought to surface factual and provocative insights in regard to the ideology of Islam and the powerful truths of God's Word. He brings clarity and reassurance of Biblical truth in light of the great deceptions of Islam's opposing doctrine and ideology. Full of information this is a must read that will both educate and enrich its reader especially in an hour where it's needed most. In addition, Dr. Gwynn has brought into perspective a wonderful overview of our faith and exposed those determined to undermine those very Judeo-Christian foundations of our faith and culture that has made our nation great. This book is a startlingly clear vision of it all!

–Bruce W. Assaf
Founder Blow the Trumpet, Int.
Author of:
Behind The Veil of Radical Islam The Coming War
If My People

Conflict
Christianity's Love vs Islam's Submission

Also by Dr. Gwynn

Anything for Acceptance

The President Was a Good Man

Easter – Not what you think!

Chrislam – What Communion Hath Light With Darkness?

Healing – The Children's Bread

The gods Among Us

Created to Live

Conflict
Christianity's Love vs Islam's Submission

Dr. Murl Edward Gwynn

Published by MEG Enterprises Publications
PO Box 2165
Reidsville, GA 30453
(912) 557-6507
meg@kencable.net
www.murlgwynn.com

Unless otherwise identified, Scripture quotations are from
the Holy Bible New International Version, copyright ©
1973, 1978, 1984 by International Bible Society. Zondervan
Publishing House. Used by permission.

Scripture quotations marked KJV are from the King James
Version of the Bible.

Unless otherwise noted, quotations from the Quran are from
the *The Holy Qur'an,* English Translation, Translated by
Abdullah Yusuf Ali, 2000 edition by Wordsmith Editions
Limited, 8B East Street, Ware, Hertfordshire SG 12 9H.

Printed in the U.S.A

ISBN: 978-0-9711766-8-3

TABLE OF CONTENTS

ACKNOWLEDGMENTS

Ruth, my wonderful wife.

SSG Darren P Hubbell, Sr. who died for freedom's cause in Iraq, June 20, 2007.

Father, Son, and Holy Spirit for my eternal life through Messiah Jesus!

PREFACE

I came to write this book after sixty-five years of life, thirty nine spent in the service of our Lord Jesus. Obviously, I am not an expert of all there is to know about Christianity or Islam. Most of what I know about Christianity has come by way of life's experience and walking with our Lord according to Holy Scripture. What I know about Islam has come through study, research, observations of the world, and the media. By no means do any of these sources complete my knowledge of the subject of this book. Time will tell and bring full completion to my studies, just as it will to all who diligently search for truth.

This book came about through my studies to earn a doctor of theology degree. In the course of my studies, it troubled me that the Christian population of the United States was unaware of the attack of Islamic thinking that is invading much of society. The Church seems to be asleep to the dangers to their faith and to the long range effects Islam can have on Christian truth.

This book is a wake-up, a warning, and a reminder to all those who desire to see Christianity understood for the loving and life changing reality it is. This book desires to focus attention on the efficacy of Christianity and its ability to bring a person to the truth.

It is important to keep in mind that any comments about either Christianity or Islam are not meant to demean or belittle any person or people who believe differently than me.

CHAPTER 1

INTRODUCTION

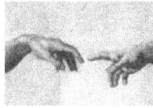

I can remember the day as if it were yesterday; it was a clear, bright, and beautiful September 11, 2001, day. The roads and interstate to Brunswick, Georgia, were full of people driving to their destinations of fun, relaxation, or business just like any other day of the week. Many travelers were coming to Florida and the many vacation sites that dot one of the most popular states in the United States. Many, as usual, were on their way to work or meetings like I was in Georgia. We all were unaware, if we didn't have our radios on in our cars, that something of the worst kind had taken place in New York City, Pennsylvania, and Washington, D.C.

When I arrived at Christian Renewal Church in Brunswick and entered the main auditorium, I found silence except for the video projector illuminating the upper screens on the wall with reports and pictures of New York City under attack. I was in shock! I was angry with those who would scream, *Allah is Great* as they saw the end results of those who would do such a terrible thing. I couldn't believe that anyone would hate the United Sates of America that much. I would soon learn, however, that there are many in the world that would cause the deaths of thousands of people just because they wouldn't adhere to their beliefs.

The year 2008 our nation elected the first African-American President in its history. President Barack Obama was born and raised by a white mother and a black African father of Muslim religious background. President Obama professes Christianity as his religious affiliation. Needless to say, the United States of America is very interested in the Muslim association of our president and how that affects his decisions and what that would mean to our nation as a whole.

This book is not about our president or his religious convictions; our president's association with Islam is mentioned only to bring thought of the time in history we find ourselves. The twenty-first century is a time of turmoil, financial upheaval, and social change as never before. There are wars, rumors of wars, earthquakes, global climate changes and many other disheartening things affecting most everything people hold dear.

One of those disheartening things that affect our world generally is the rise of Islamic extremists who promote terror in most nations. Although religious extremism has sprouted at times throughout history, the last two decades have seen a rise in Islamic terrorism. This Islamic terrorism was most realized with the attack on the World Trade Towers on September 11th, 2001, in New York City by nineteen terrorists who hijacked airliners and flew them into the twin towers as well as the Pentagon in Arlington, Virginia.

The convictions of Islamic terrorists have brought much attention to Islam in general and the mind set of those who profess a holy allegiance to God but prey on anyone who would not adhere to their way of thinking. In other words, confusion exists over what distinguishes peaceful religions from ones focused upon war. The world is seeing those who would kill if others do not submit, and for the most part, those who are docile about their religious convictions and would permit just about anything. There is a collision of thought and deeds.

The attack by Islamic terrorists on the World Trade Towers, the Pentagon, and the airliner that crashed in Pennsylvania claimed the lives of 2,973 victims and injured over 6,000, including nationals from more than seventy countries.[1] Within days of the attack, many churches throughout the world were flooded with people seeking God and trying to make sense of the whole bloody event. At the National Cathedral on September 14th, 2001, President George W. Bush and other national and international dignitaries prayed, gave speeches, and helped the United States of America mourn the loss of the many victims. Obviously, no one present at the cathedral that day thought of the terrorists as honorable people, but many did proclaim Islam as a peaceful religion. While a whole religious group of people can not be blamed for the actions of those nineteen extremists, there seemed to be a nagging connection with those who destroy under the cry, "Allah

---

[1] Sean Alfano, "Grim Milestone for U.S. Soldiers Killed in Iraq," *Afghanistan CBS News* Washington, Sept. 22, 2006, http://www.cbsnews.com/stories/2006/09/22/terror/main2035427.shtml (accessed April 15, 2010).

Akbar (God is great!)" with those who do similar things throughout the world.

Christianity was founded, if one can say Christianity was founded, upon the Judaic spiritual beliefs. Its history can be traced back to the very beginning of creation; I will discuss this further in the chapters to come. Judaic and Christian Scriptures tell of bloodshed and many extreme examples of people responding to God's call under strong convictions that led them to believe that what they were doing was sanctioned by God. We see that these convictions have not changed over the thousands of years of history. People still cry out in adoration to God as they behead someone who thinks differently then they do.

This book will, I hope, bring insight and understanding of our times and what we believe. Belief, you see, can cause us to do many things: defend something we hold dear, respond with determined conviction, and outright get upset if others differ. Too often we fail to examine or think through what and why we believe what we believe. No human is immune from improper or incorrect responses to others when something we hold dear is challenged. If what we hold dear is not founded upon biblical and righteous truths, it doesn't matter because our inner desire to be correct will usually outweigh any truth.

The events of history are speeding along at a pace that most humans can't even imagine. We can send a message to someone thousands of miles away and receive a reply in less then a minute or two. The internet and email make it possible for us to see the events of the day flashing before our eyes. It doesn't matter if those events have to do with government or religion, it doesn't matter if they are true or not, it still comes into our homes and informs us and will mold our thinking if we are not wise and understanding of their source and purpose.

Many of those things that come into our homes have to do with religion or in some way touched upon religion; we just don't realize to what degree. Especially now in the twenty-first century we are realizing religious implications as never before. Whether we like it or not, the earth is being bombarded by spiritual realities that impact just about everything we hold close.

Christianity, for the most part, has been the dominant religion in the world until the latter part of the twentieth century. Most of the greater economic countries of the world were in one way or the other touched by the Christian and Judaic beliefs. The importance of freedom demands that everyone has a chance to make his or her own way and to find God through his or her own convictions.

Christianity, however, as it is being realized, has become complacent and asleep to the very truths we were supposed to declare and live. That is why we find Christianity on the decline in the Western nations. Our nation, and for that matter, churches have given into a political correctness (PC) that prevents us from speaking the truth and declaring its power.

Islam in two forms (Sunni and Shiite) is spreading throughout the world at a rate that is surpassing other religions by leaps and bounds. Different sources quoted by Ontario Consultants on Religious Tolerance view the Islamic growth rates as surpassing Christianity in general:

- The growth rate of Islam, according to the U.S. Center for World Mission, at 2.9% is higher than the 2.6% growth rate of the world's population. Thus, the percentage of Muslims in the world is growing on the order of 0.6% per year.
- Futurist John Gary stated in 1997 that Islam is the fastest-growing of the major world religions. This is driven by the higher birth rates in the third world.
- Barrett & Johnson's estimated in an article in the International Bulletin of Missionary Research that the number of Muslims would grow from 1.22 billion in the year 2000 to 1.89 billion by 2025.
- Author Samuel Huntington predicts that "Muslims in the world will continue to increase dramatically, amounting to 20

percent of the world's population about the turn of the [21st] century, surpassing the number of Christians some years later..."[2]

Emory C. Bogle in his book, *Islam Origin & Belief,* states that *"The dynamics of Islam's growth and invigorating experimental ideologies qualify it as one of the most influential forces in contemporary times."*[3]

With this in mind, there is no wonder that Islam is demanding our attention and forcing the so called Christian nations to take notice. We can't deny that something is developing in the world that could and probably will change many traditions, standards, and long held beliefs. The time for sitting on our laurels is gone. There must be a re-awakening of those principles that made America great and evangelistic.

It grieves this servant of the one true God that we seem to be more interested in financial economy but deny or simply overlook the spiritual economy of our nation. We have made finances the one and only value of our time at

[2] B.A. Robinson, "Growth Rate of Christianity & Islam," *Religious Tolerance*, Nov. 6, 2001, http://www.religioustolerance.org/growth_isl_chr.htm (accessed April 23, 2010).

[3] Emory C. Bogle, *Islam Origin & Belief* (Austin, TX: University of Texas Press, 1998), xi.

the expense of true riches that will go with us into eternity if we will walk with God. Maybe, just maybe, we need the awakening of our personal and corporate souls by an outside source such as Islam.

Islam and those who adhere to its tenets do not seem to waver in their religious fervor or dogged patronage to their beliefs. Wherever one finds Muslims, one finds a collective gathering of like-minded citizens who rally around one common theme: Allah, the Koran and Mohammed. These three pillars of Islam are the foundation and unmoving cement that keeps each Muslim joined together with their community. One could say that if one of those pillars could be discredited, Islam would fail. This will not happen until the true Messiah, Jesus the Christ, returns to Earth and declares the real from the false.

The truth of the matter comes down to just that: the true Messiah's revelation and the climax of history. When we come to the bare meat of history and holiness, we will see what God does through His Son and His bride, the Church. No one will be immune to God's final workings, and no one will be able to hide from the dark days coming upon the earth. There are forces, however, at work trying to change the outcome of these events.

The battles and testing that are taking place and will take place find their beginnings long before any attack on buildings or nations. Thousands of years before modern nations and peoples went to the moon, the first steps of conflict were in the making. Abraham of the Bible left his home and relatives to go to a country God informed him of. He made inroads with peoples and places and did things that tested his beliefs and fortified his faith with deeds. His love and trust in the God who called him would only be made strong through obedience, but failure was always possible. Nevertheless, Abraham went into history, human as he was and weak as the rest of us, and, in the vernacular of our time, "did his thing!" His thing would end up being the one thing that we now in this century must deal with.

The thing, or should I say persons, we must deal with are those who profess Ishmael as their ancestral father, the son of Abraham through his wife Sarai's maid, Hagar. Ishmael, as Muslims claim, but can not be proved from history or archeology, is the father of all the non-Hebrew tribes to this day, the tribes that now believe in Allah and disbelieve in the God of Abraham, Isaac and Jacob. This student believes that our future spiritual battles and worldly events that will touch even time itself will have to do with those who profess to be descendants of Ishmael.[4] It is important to keep in mind: there is no historical evidence that proves that Ishmael is the father of the Muslim peoples. However, I believe the Muslims and their Islamic thinking is the spirit of conflict that was demonstrated in Ishmael.

> *And the angel of the Lord said unto her, I will multiply thy seed exceedingly, that it shall not be numbered for multitude. And the angel of the Lord said unto her, Behold, thou art with child, and shalt bear a son, and shalt call his name Ishmael; because the Lord hath heard thy affliction. And he will be a wild man; his hand will be against every man, and every man's hand against him; and he shall dwell in the presence of all his brethren.*
>
> Gen 16:10-12 KJV

What will the Church of the Living God do about these things? How will we respond when our sacred beliefs are trampled under foot? Will the Church stand up and declare the clarion cry that prompts faith and fortitude? Is there efficacy in what the Christian Scriptures teach and declare to be the Word of God? Does what we the Church believe go deep enough to enforce our creeds, strengthen

---

[4] Gn. 16:1-12

our faith, and motivate us to take a stand even in the face of persecution?

Scripture calls us to trust, test, and abide. Our beliefs must be founded upon faith in God and trusting Him no matter what. We must test the spirits and any system or decree that is contrary to Scripture or that denies or proclaims something that is outside of the Bible. Our determination to walk with God and our resolve to be molded

> *We must trust, test & abide!*

into the image of Jesus require that we abide in God's word, will, and Spirit. Abiding is the everyday thing that makes our religion more than a Sunday routine and motivates us to action. Action is permitting the sanctifying process of the Holy Spirit and denying the world and its ways to mold us in its image. Only through these realities will we be able to recognize false religions when they threaten our world and our personal beliefs.

Islam denies that God has a son.[5] It stands totally against everything Christianity stands for. It is a world religion that is now at the forefront of world thought and economy. It does not change to sweeten its appeal nor does

---

[5] Surah. 4:171.

it permit any lenience for those who deny its foundations. The only truth Muslims believe is their pillars of faith, the Koran, the prophet Mohammed, and Allah. They do not accept Christianity in any form, and they will never bow to the Christian God.

I will show through this writing the efficacy of the Christian faith and the weakness of Islam. I will open holy Hebraic and Christian Scripture so as to help us make an informed choice. The choice will not necessarily be between Christianity and Islam but the choice to walk with God as He would have us walk. Jesus told us, *"Come unto me, all ye that labor and are heavy laden, and I will give you rest!"*[6] If we refuse or fail to seek out God's will and ways, we will fail to recognize the darkness in this world and those from whom it will come. It is the duty of every Christian to rest in Jesus, stop laboring for those things that will not pass into eternity, and be about God's plan.

The legacy of the Christian faith is founded upon thousands and thousands who have gone on before us. We have a heritage of wonderful examples that stood the test of time and danger. We must not permit ourselves to become complacent nor lazy with what we believe. What we believe is glorious. The truths of God that have been passed

---

[6] Matt. 11:28.

down to us are unmatchless. We must not sit idly by and do nothing; we must know, kneel, and declare.

There are many in the Christian family that do what is necessary and proclaim the message of Christ to Muslims throughout the world. Many have paid with their lives, men like Kim Sun-il of South Korea whose desire was to be a missionary to the Muslims in Iraq. He went to Iraq and worked for the Gana General Trading Co., a South Korean company. A lover of Jesus with a missionary's heart, Kim fell into the hands of Islamic terrorists on June 22, 2004, who beheaded him not only for his support of the American military in Iraq but for being a Christian. After the beheading, many Islamic clerics boasted that Kim Sun-il was an infidel who should not have been in Iraq.[7] This account of the martyred Kim Sun-il is one of many and will continue until Jesus returns to Earth.

We can see from these sorts of things that Islam creates a mindset that is very contrary and foreign to the Christian way of thinking and worshipping. Some may say that those Muslims who commit such terrible acts in the name of their god are the exception and not the rule. Some

---

[7] Catherine Donaldson, "South Korea Confirms Hostage Killed," *Fox News.com*, June 23, 2004, http://www.foxnews.com/story/0,2933,123343,00.html (accessed April 24, 2010.

may say that most Muslims do not believe in nor promote acts of violence and live peaceable lives. I would agree with those assumptions and also believe that most Muslims just want to live a life of peace and happiness. However, Islam's teachings, if followed according to what is written and propagated, can only create an attitude and atmosphere of evil. If one thinks about it, those who are seen as extremist are really the best adherents of Islam for they follow the letter of their scripture as well as the spirit of it. In the following chapters I will give more details that lead me to these conclusions.

As I have stated earlier, the United States of America is being bombarded with a spirit of political correctness (PC). This PC does not have any room for common sense nor does it consider history, Biblical truth, and sacred foundations. There seems to be a lack of good and an attitude of selfishness. Our nation can't seem to get past money and materialism and see that the most important things in life are not of this Earth. When one speaks of rightness about any subject, one must be careful that what one says does not hurt someone else's feelings. Those things that society used to think of as evil are now being thought of as good and vice versa.[8] It is a trap that

---

[8] Isa. 5:20.

most people have fallen into. Our schools have taught subjects that deny God and His creation. They have moved away from teaching subjects that help upcoming citizens stand alert and astute to science and social awareness. The end test of subjects have become more important then the subject itself. Many youngsters graduate with little ability to read or write. Writing in itself is almost forgotten, and in its place, computers and handheld music devices have prevailed. The need of the average American child to be glued to the T.V. or computer has far surpassed the joy of reading a good book. These things in general promote an attitude of lethargy and then become the avenue whereby false religions and their dangers grow. When a nation becomes self centered or can't recognize the social and spiritual dangers advancing toward them, its citizens become prey for any system that will live what it promotes, even if that system promotes death.

Death is one of the avenues that Islam promotes. Chief Palestinian Authority cleric Mufti Sheikh Ikrimeh Sabri stated,

We tell them, in as much as you love life, the Muslim loves death and martyrdom. There is a great difference between he who loves the

"*The Muslim loves death and martyrdom.*"

hereafter and he who loves this world. The Muslim loves death and [strives for] martyrdom.[9]

It is no wonder that America does not understand those who would destroy in the name of god. We have become complacent and dulled by money, luxury and greed and have gotten away from our Judaic and Christian traditions and beliefs. Because we are being taught that we must not judge, we will be judged by our own standards, which are weak at best. Our standards pale in comparison with those who deem death more important than life. Christians should be livid about statements like Mufti Sheikh Ikrimeh Sabri made, that rage should be tempered by love.

Christianity is by spiritual nature the only religion based on love, for God is love. Its foundation has everything to do with an unselfish attitude and promotes others as more important than self. It is these truths that must prevail as we advance into history facing the many forms and systems of evil. If Christians don't recognize the Anti-Christ spirit that is invading all the systems and societies of this world, there is no hope for the

---

[9] Steven Stalinsky, "Dealing in Death," *The Middle East Media Research*, May 24, 2004. http://old.nationalreview.com/comment/stalinsky200405240846.asp (accessed April 24, 2010).

17

proclamation of truth. Everything and anything that denies Jesus as the Messiah comes from the anti-Christ. This is not something new; it has always been in the world. We were warned thousands of years ago that the spirit of Anti-Christ would come and is in the world.[10] This author believes that Islam is now, in these later days, the modern face of the Anti-Christ spirit in the earth today. It will be the main power that mankind must deal with and make decisions about. There will not be any sitting on the side lines and hoping it will not touch me as each person will be drawn into the Anti-Christ web. Either we will profess Jesus as Lord or we will fall to the spirit that denies Messiah Jesus altogether. I will discuss the Anti-Christ and the Muslim belief in a coming Imam Mahdi (the guided one) who will profess to be Christ in Appendix A.

This book is titled *Conflict – Christianity's Love vs. Islam's Submission,* and as such, there must be some evidence that supports that belief. Either the Christian belief has the power to change lives and keep the believer on a righteous keel or it doesn't. There can not be any fanciful ideas or sloppy theology that draws someone to the cross of Christ. Historical events alone will never keep someone on the straight and narrow; there must be

---

[10] 1Jn. 4:2-3

something alive and real for someone to accept and then walk in its power to change lives. Christianity isn't a religion in the historical sense; it is a relationship with God Himself through His Son. The only way someone will know the power of the indwelling God is by a total surrender to Love Himself. The God of the Jew is the God of the Christian and as such is the Father of the Lord Jesus. As we study the great depth and cost God went to demonstrate His love for mankind, we will find that Christianity truly has the efficacy that is necessary to change lives.

CHAPTER 2

BEGINNINGS

As we discus the efficacy of Christian love compared to Islam's submission, we must know from whence each came. Most people believe that Christianity started after the death and resurrection of Jesus the Nazarene; actually, it had its roots in the Garden of Eden. Those who were called Christians first received that title at Antioch around the year 34 AD,[1] but the foundation of Christianity has its beginnings in Genesis.

When Adam and Eve sinned, God told them that the offspring of Eve would one day be the human who would crush (bruise) Satan's head.[2] We see from this first reference that a son (he) would come and crush Satan's power over mankind. That and many other references in Scripture speak of the Messiah, or the "son," who would crush the head of Satan.

> *he will crush your head..,*

---

[1] Ac. 11:36.

[2] Gn. 3:15.

Any astute student of the Bible would recognize that Jesus not only fulfilled that promise but that He could be realized in each book of the Bible:

- *In Genesis, Jesus Christ is the seed of the woman.*
- *In Exodus, He is the Passover lamb.*
- *In Leviticus, He is our high priest.*
- *In Numbers, He is the pillar of cloud by day and the pillar of fire by night.*
- *In Deuteronomy, He is the prophet like unto Moses.*
- *In Joshua, He is the captain of our salvation.*
- *In Judges, He is our judge and lawgiver.*
- *In Ruth, He is our kinsman redeemer.*
- *In 1st and 2nd Samuel, He is our trusted prophet.*
- *In Kings and Chronicles, He is our reigning king.*
- *In Ezra, He is the rebuilder of the broken down walls of human life.*
- *In Esther, He is our Mordecai.*
- *In Job, He is our ever-living redeemer.*
- *In Psalms, He is our shepherd.*
- *In Proverbs and Ecclesiastes, He is our wisdom.*
- *In the Song of Solomon, He is the loving bridegroom.*
- *In Isaiah, He is the prince of peace.*
- *In Jeremiah, He is the righteous branch.*
- *In Lamentations, He is our weeping prophet.*

- *In Ezekiel, He is the wonderful four-faced man.*
- *In Daniel, He is the fourth man in life's "fiery furnace."*
- *In Hosea, He is the faithful husband, forever married to the backslider.*
- *In Joel, He is the baptizer with the Holy Ghost and fire.*
- *In Amos, He is our burden-bearer.*
- *In Obadiah, He is the mighty one to save.*
- *In Jonah, He is our great foreign missionary.*
- *In Micah, He is the messenger of beautiful feet.*
- *In Nahum, He is the avenger of God's elect.*
- *In Habakkuk, He is God's evangelist, crying, "revive thy work in the midst of the years."*
- *In Zephaniah, He is our Saviour.*
- *In Haggai, He is the restorer of God's lost heritage.*
- *In Zechariah, He is the fountain opened up in the house of David for sin and uncleanness.*
- *In Malachi, He is the Sun of Righteousness, rising with healing in His wings.*
- *In Matthew, He is King of the Jews.*
- *In Mark, He is the Servant.*
- *In Luke, He is the Son of Man, feeling what you feel.*
- *In John, He is the Son of God.*
- *In Acts, He is the Savior of the world.*

- *In Romans, He is the righteousness of God.*
- *In I Corinthians, He is the Rock that followed Israel.*
- *In II Corinthians, He is the Triumphant One, giving victory.*
- *In Galatians, He is your liberty; He sets you free.*
- *In Ephesians, He is Head of the Church.*
- *In Philippians, He is your joy.*
- *In Colossians, He is your completeness.*
- *In 1st and 2nd Thessalonians, He is your hope.*
- *In I Timothy, He is your faith.*
- *In II Timothy, He is your stability.*
- *In Philemon, He is your Benefactor.*
- *In Titus, He is truth.*
- *In Hebrews, He is your perfection.*
- *In James, He is the Power behind your faith.*
- *In I Peter, He is your example.*
- *In II Peter, He is your purity.*
- *In I John, He is your life.*
- *In II John, He is your pattern.*
- *In III John, He is your motivation.*
- *In Jude, He is the foundation of your faith.*
- *In Revelation, He is your coming King.*[3]

This insight of the "son of Adam" who would come and set straight those things that Adam failed at is not some

[3] Scrib.com. *Jesus in Every Book of the Bible* http://www.scribd.com/doc/40663295/Jesus-in-Every-Book-of-the-Bible (accessed February 8, 2011).

fanciful thinking on the part of this author. If we accept the authenticity of the Bible, it is easy to see the importance and power that each book of the Bible portrays Jesus as. In the New Testament and the book of Matthew, we read the following:

The book of the generation of Jesus Christ, the son of David, the son of Abraham. Abraham begat Isaac; and Isaac begat Jacob; and Jacob begat Judas and his brethren; And Judas begat Phares and Zara of Thamar; and Phares begat Esrom; and Esrom begat Aram; And Aram begat Aminadab; and Aminadab begat Naasson; and Naasson begat Salmon; And Salmon begat Boaz of Rachab; and Boaz begat Obed of Ruth; and Obed begat Jesse; And Jesse begat David the king; and David the king begat Solomon of her that had been the wife of Urias; And Solomon begat Roboam; and Roboam begat Abia; and Abia begat Asa; And Asa begat Josaphat; and Josaphat begat Joram; and Joram begat Ozias; And Ozias begat Joatham; and Joatham begat Achaz; and Achaz begat Ezekias; And Ezekias begat Manasses; and Manasses begat Amon; and Amon begat Josias; And Josias begat Jechonias and his brethren, about the time they were carried away to Babylon: And after they were brought to Babylon, Jechonias begat Salathiel; and Salathiel begat Zorobabel; And Zorobabel begat Abiud; and Abiud begat Eliakim; and Eliakim begat Azor; And Azor begat Sadoc;

and Sadoc begat Achim; and Achim begat Eliud; And Eliud begat Eleazar; and Eleazar begat Matthan; and Matthan begat Jacob; And Jacob begat Joseph the husband of Mary, of whom was born Jesus, who is called Christ. So all the generations from Abraham to David are fourteen generations; and from David until the carrying away into Babylon are fourteen generations; and from the carrying away into Babylon unto Christ are fourteen generations.

Matthew 1:1-17

Jesus is the son of Adam, Abraham, Isaac and Jacob and the rest of His lineage as stated in Scripture. The lineage proves that the promise given to Adam of a coming son who would crush Satan's head is fulfilled in Jesus the son of Mary. He is the "seed" that God was speaking of when He told Satan that *"he will crush your head"* in the Garden of Eden.[4] Even Jesus Himself declared Himself to be the one who was to come and redeem mankind: *"Think not that I am come to destroy the law, or the prophets: I am not come to destroy, but to fulfill."*[5] Also in Hebrews 10:7-8, Jesus stated that the Scripture spoke of Himself.[6]

---

[4] Gn. 3:15.

[5] Matt. 5:17.

[6] "In the volume of the book it is written of me." Hebrews 10:7-8.

Herbert Lockyer in his classic, *All the Messianic Prophecies of the Bible*, states, *"Our Lord is found in the Word, that is, in the letter; the Word is found in Him, in the life. Because of the identity of the written Word with the living Word, faith in the infallibility of the former is essential to the revelation and authority of latter."*[7] Jesus, then, is not only realized in His person amongst those who witnessed Him first hand but can be realized through the written word passed down to us.

I dwell on the fall of man and promise of the coming Messiah in Genesis, not only for its spiritual importance, but for its historical importance. The promise of a Messiah or Son who would crush the head of Satan took place around 4000 BC.[8] Although no one could know the exact time of Adam's sin and fall, the four thousand year frame would be close. No matter what the exact date, I use the general time element to show that the promise of a coming one who would be mankind's redeemer was well

[7] Herbert Lockyer, *All The Messianic Prophecies Of The Bible* (Grand Rapids, MI: Zondervan Publishing House, 1973), 25.

[8] Ed. R. Meelhuysen, "Dating Creation and Understanding the Jubilee Calendar,"*Bible Plus* 1993-2008, http://www.bibleplus.org/creation/datingcreation.htm (accessed April 24, 2010).

before any religious writings and specifically the Koran of the Muslims.

The Koran came by way of Mohammed in oral tradition around 610 AD to the eighth century when it was put into the improved Arabic script.[9] The Koran's accuracy, when quoting Hebraic and Christian Scripture, contains many mistakes and could never be used to help someone know God, much less understand who Jesus of Nazareth is.

Christianity looks back at the person of Jesus through the many prophecies of the Hebrew Scripture about the coming Messiah. The events of history that Scripture speaks of and the dealings of the Hebrew Jews can not be taken for granted, nor have they come about by happenstance. If what we find in Scripture is also found in the textbook of history, we must be wise and consider their importance. Not only is the Messiah and the events of His death and resurrection spoken about in Scripture, they are confirmed by historians like Flavius Josephus.

Josephus lived from around 37 AD to 100 AD and was a historian for the Jews and Romans of his day. In his historical writings he not only writes from information received from outside sources, he also writes from personal

---

[9] Alan Jones, *The Koran Introduction, xx*. London: Phoenix, a division of the Orion Publishing Group Ltd., 2001.

observation; however, he was not an observer of Jesus' life. His writings have been accepted by most scholars and Christian historians. What makes Josephus important to the Christian researcher is his mention of Jesus who was *"condemned... to the cross..."* in his *Antiquities of the Jews,* Book XVIII, Chapter III.[10]

Archaeology over the past 60 years has given mankind much evidence to support the Biblical authenticity of Jesus and the places and events recorded by His disciples. The Dead Sea Scrolls, which were discovered along the northwest shore of the Dead Sea between 1947 and 1956, proved not only Hebrew Scripture, but through the Isaiah Scroll contains some of the most dramatic messianic prophecies. The Dead Sea Scrolls, which date back to 100 – 200 BC, comprise the oldest group of Old Testament manuscripts ever found and give absolute evidence of the Messiah.[11] Jesus fulfilled the prophecies that the book of Isaiah stated the Messiah must do.

Archaeology also gives us another find that confirms not only the accuracy of the Bible but proves the

---

[10] William Whiston, *The Works of Flavius Josephus,* IV (Grand Rapids, MI: Baker Book House, 1979), 11.

[11] Randall Niles, "Dead Sea Scrolls – A Compelling Find," *All About Archaeology,* http://www.allaboutarchaeology.org/dead-sea-scrolls.htm (accessed May 23, 2010).

predating of anything Islam has that would try to convince us of the Bible's inaccuracies. *The New York Times* on July 26, 2006, carried an article titled "Book Buried in Irish Bog Is Called a Major Find" The article stated,

> *Ireland's National Museum said on Wednesday that a 1,200-year-old Book of Psalms found last week by a construction worker in a bog was so archaeologically significant that it could be called an "Irish equivalent to the Dead Seas Scrolls...the book was found open at a page showing Psalm 83 in Latin...Psalm 83 exhorts God to act against conspirator nations plotting to wipe out "the name of Israel."*[12]

The book found in the bog helps to confirm that the Scripture we know today is accurate and reliable.

Although the many biblical writers did not intend to provide mankind with a guidebook to the places of Jesus' trek in life, they nevertheless gave us factual evidence that proved His existence and reality. I mention one in particular; places like the Church of the Holy Sepulcher, built between 326 AD and 335 AD, have become an accepted place of both Golgotha and the Empty Tomb of

---

[12] Alan Cowell, "Book Buried in Irish Bog Is Called a Major Find," *The New York Times*, July 27, 2006, http://www.nytimes.com/2006/07/27/books/27psal.html (accessed June 6, 2010).

Jesus' sufferings.[13] There is more and more evidence from archaeology being unearthed year after year that substantiates authenticity of Jesus' life and message.

There are many other historical and undisputable facts of Jesus' life and ministry, but there will always be skeptics. Muslim teaching does not deny the historical Jesus of the Bible; it just denies the most sacred truths surrounding His life and divinity. Probably one of the main reasons for their denial is because those truths come by way of the Jew. Islam

There is no proof of Muhammad being descended from Ishmael.

will not receive anything from the Hebrew Jew; could it be that Isaac (from his lineage comes the Jew) and Ishmael (from Ishmael's lineage the Muslims believe they are descendants) are in conflict to this day? (There is no Biblical, historical or archeological evidence of the Muslim's claims of being descended from Ishmael. See Appendix C.) These two men, sons of Abraham, one by way of Abraham's wife, Isaac, and the other, Ishmael, by way of her servant girl, were in constant agitation from birth. One was considered the son of promise and the other

---

[13] Richard Bauckham *et al.*, *Jesus 2000* (Oxford, England: Lion Publishing plc, 1989).

a usurper. Without the Jew, however, we have no Messianic Jesus! The Koran teaches that Muslims should curse their enemy, the Jew; it states in Surah 9:30, *"...Allah's Curse be on them, how they are deluded away from the truth!"[14]*

God's purpose was to bring the testimony of Himself through the offspring of Abraham, Jacob. Jacob's name was changed by God to Israel, and his offspring are the Jews.[15] God chose Israel to teach all nations of Himself and to witness to the existence of the one true living God.[16] Through Israel came the holy writings, the promises of God, and the Redeemer. From the holy writings and the seven feasts (see chart),[17] which God called Israel to celebrate, we find Him keeping the Jew from assimilating into the norm of the world. The Jew was to be a special people to keep the testimony of the one true God in the earth and to proclaim the coming of the Messiah.[18]

---

[14] Surah. 9:30

[15] Gn. 32:28.

[16] Isa. 43:1-12.

[17] Ceil Rosen, *Christ in the Passover* (Chicago, Il: Moody Press, 1978) 12-13.

[18] Dt. 7:6.

Feast	Temporal Significance for Israel under the Law	Future Significance for all God's people under Grace	Scripture	Event
PASSOVER	Redemption from bondage in Egypt	Believers in Christ redeemed from bondage of sin	1 Peter 1:18-19	THE CRUCIFIXION (Redemption)
UNLEAVENED BREAD	Purging of all leaven (symbol of sin)	All believers in Christ cleansed from sin and empowered to walk in newness of life.	1 Cor 5:7 2 Cor 5:21	(Sanctification) (Justification)
FIRSTFRUITS	Thanksgiving for first fruits the promise of the harvest to come (first of the grain presented to God)	Christ, the First to rise from the dead – the promise of resurrection and eternal life for all who believe on Him.	1 Cor 15:20-22	THE RESURRECTION OF CHRIST
FEAST OF WEEKS (Pentecost)	Thanksgiving for first harvest and (according to oral tradition, the time of giving of the Law at Sinai)	God's first harvest of those redeemed in Christ God's Law written on the hearts of the redeemed.	Acts 2:1-4 Heb 10:16	THE COMING OF THE HOLY SPIRIT AND THE BIRTH OF THE CHURCH
FEAST OF TRUMPETS	A solemn assembly (trumpets blown to prepare for the Day of Atonement)	The beginning of the regathering of Israel to the land in preparation for the final Day of Atonement	Jer 32:37 1 Thess 4:16-17	ISRAEL REGATHERED THE RETURN OF CHRIST

		The assembly of all believers, dead and alive, in the heavens with Christ.		
DAY OF ATONEMENT	A solemn assembly for repentance and forgiveness under the Law (repeated annually)	Believers in Christ forgiven by one atonement for all time

The rest of Israel will repent and look to her Messiah | Heb 9:28

Zech 12:10 | ISRAEL TURNS TO HER MESSIAH |
| FEAST OF BOOTHS | Harvest celebration and memorial of tabernacles in the wilderness | Joyous assembly – all peoples brought under the rule of the King Messiah | Zech 14:16 | THE KINGDOM OF GOD ON EARTH |

Robert G. Evans in his book, *The Seven Messianic Festivals,* sums up the festivals in the following way:

> *To Christians, the seven festivals of ancient Israel all point to Christ, who was crucified on Passover; lay buried on the Unleavened Bread; rose from the dead on First Fruits; and sent the Holy Spirit on Pentecost.* [19]

As one studies the Old Testament, one can see the fulfillment in the New Testament pertaining to the Messiah, or the son of Adam. The following list, which shows us the parallels of the Old and New Testament, is taken from Dr.

[19] Robert Evans. *The Seven Messianic Festivals,* (Columbus, GA: Brentwood Christian Press, 2001), 208.

Mark A. Gabriel's book, *Jesus and Muhammad Profound Differences and Surprising Similarities.* Dr. Gabriel grew up as a devout Muslim but now is a practicing Christian.

Old Testament	*New Testament*

Jesus is the seed of Abraham.
Gn. 22:18, 49:10   Matt. 1:1-16
Isa. 11:1

Jesus is from the house of Jesse.
Isa. 11:1, 10   Matt. 1:5-16

Jesus is born in Bethlehem.
Mic. 5:2   Matt. 2:1

Jesus is born from a virgin.
Isa. 7:14   Lk. 1:26-33

Jesus was called from Egypt.
Hos. 11:1   Matt. 2:14-15

Jesus' ministry, humility, and miracles.
Isa. 35:4-6   Matt. 11:28-30
Isa. 42:1-4   Matt. 11:2-5

Jesus is savior of the world.
Gn. 3:15   Matt. 18:11
          Lk. 19:10
          Jn. 12:47

Jesus enters Jerusalem riding a mule.
Zec. 9:9   Matt. 21:7-11

Jesus was betrayed.

Zec. 11:12-13   Matt. 27:3_8

Jesus left alone and the fleeing of the disciples.
Isa. 53:1-3   Matt. 25:56

Jesus remains silent during his trial and dies for
the world's salvation.
Isa. 53:4-8   Matt. 26:63
                                 Matt. 27:14
                                 Jn. 18:14

Jesus during the events of the crucifixion.
Isa. 50:6   Matt. 26:67
Ps. 22:1-18   Matt. 27:26, 35, 3
Ps. 69:21   Mat. 27: 46, 48

Jesus is crucified between two thieves and buried
in a rich man's tomb.
Isa. 53:9   Matt. 27:38, 57-60

Jesus rises from the dead and frees the souls of
those who died in hope of resurrection.
Ps. 16:10   Matt. 28:5-7
Ps. 24:7-10   1 Pe. 3:19[20]

As I have stated earlier, the scriptural and historical writings give ample evidence of the person of Messiah found in Jesus, or the son of Adam who was promised to come. If one will accept these things as fact, one must come to the conclusion that Jesus is the Messiah, and if so,

---

[20] Mark A. Gabriel, *Jesus and Muhammad: Profound Differences and Surprising Similarities*, (Lake Mary, FL: Frontline, A Strange Company, 2004), 234-236.

Christianity really began with the promise of Adam's offspring who would redeem the world.

Why would this be so important? It is important because if Jesus truly is the promised *"son"* to come, then everything spoken about him through history far surpasses any writings about another redeemer to come. No religion or faith has the power to changes lives as the Christian belief in Jesus of Nazareth who is the Messiah of God.

These facts set the stage for belief and understanding in the one true God. The prophets in the Old and New Testaments spoke of the coming Messiah. Their messages were confirmed after years of waiting and in many cases fulfilled to the exact day. The authenticity of those prophets stood the test of time and was confirmed by reliable witnesses. If their message would not have come true, they would have been considered false prophets, and their message would have died and been lost in time. But their message was confirmed and was realized in Jesus. As a matter of fact, we are told that if someone comes and brings any message that either denies that Jesus came in the flesh or the message about Him is different from those of Scripture, he or she would be a false prophet.[21] Islam

---

[21] Gal. 1:8

denies that Jesus died for mankind and that He is the final word from God.

> *And for their saying, "Verily we have slain the messiah, Jesus the son of Mary, an Apostle of God." Yet they slew him not, and they crucified him not, but they had only his likeness. And they who differed about him were in doubt concerning him: No sure knowledge had they about him, but followed only an opinion, and they did not really slay him, but God took him up to Himself.*
>
> Surah. 4:157-158

Islam's prophet, Mohammed, taught that Jesus' beginning was not divine but only human. He denied that the Jesus of the New Testament could be the one spoken about in the Garden of Eden. As a matter of fact, Muhammad disqualified himself as a true prophet of God; as it states in the Koran, Surah 29:27, only those of the lineage of Isaac or Jacob are true prophets of Allah.[22] Also, Muhammad never prophesied about anything and in his entire life never gave any predictions of the future that could be attributed to God speaking to him.

ISLAM'S BEGINNING

It is important to keep in mind as we study this section that there are no historical evidences of Islam or

---

[22] Surah. 29:27. *"And we bestowed on him Isaac and Jacob, and placed the gift of prophecy and the scripture among his posterity; ... "*

Muhammad mentioned in any accepted ancient writings before he comes into history's view. There are no Hebraic or Christian prophecies about Islam or Muhammad. As a matter of fact, Muhammad is the beginning of Islam. The book, *The Hidden Origins of Islam* edited by Karl-Heinz Ohlig and Gerd-R. Puin Ohlig, states:

> *In other words, the first two "Islamic" centuries lie in the shadows of history, and it remains inexplicable how the development of a large Islamic empire could have left behind no witnesses whatsoever, even among groups from whom we might expect such traces, such as the enemies of the Arabs, the many Byzantines known for their literary skills and output, and the Jews and Christians living under the alleged Islamic authority.[23]*

Muhammad was born in 570 AD in Mecca. His family was part of one of the largest tribes in Arab, the Quraysh. He was apparently a religious man by the time he was twenty five. In the year 610 BC he had his first so-called revelation from Gabriel and was called to be a "warner" and prophet. Most religious leaders and the common populace of his area did not accept his revelations

---

[23] Karl-Heinz Ohlig and Gerd-R. Puin. *The Hidden Origins of Islam* (Amherst, NY: Prometheus Books, 2010), 9.

until years later when he convinced them by means of the sword to accept Islam.

Muhammad came from a lineage of occult worshippers, and many Islamic historians freely publish such accounts of Muhammad's ancestry. Muhammad's grandfather, Abu Mutaleb, was a worshiper of the Jinn-devil. Abu Mutaleb tried to sacrifice his son Addullah, Muhammad's father, but his brother rescued him and saved his life. Abu Mutaleb was also a leader in the Arabian Jinn religion. Instead of

> The Jinn - fiery spirits of the desert.

sacrificing his son Addullah, Abu sacrificed a camel to the Jinn-devil. By this, it is believed that Abu Mutaleb brought influencing spirits upon the family by which Muhammad would come.

Addullah, Muhammad's father, married Amneh, a neice of Soda Bint Zehra, the main priestess of the Jinn (a fiery spirit)[24] at Mecca, which probably furthered the demonic association within the family line of Muhammad.

---

[24] *In Islam, jinns are fiery spirits (Qur'an 15:27) particularly associated with the desert. While they are disruptive of human life, they are considered worthy of being saved. A person dying in a state of great sin may be changed into a jinni in the period of a barzakh, separation or barrier.*

Mohammed was known to have suffered from trances since his childhood because Amneh, his mother, brought on him a rukhieh, or bewitching. In the rukhieh, a Kahan priest of Jinn (Kahaneh Jinn religion) brings the spirit of Jinn to a person to whom the Kahen is connected as a medium. This may explain why Amneh was able to perform occultic ceremonies upon Mohammed. Only the Kuhhan of Arabia could perform the right of "rukhieh."[25]

Children on whom a "rukhieh" was practiced suffered from many signs such as falling into trances and having convulsions. Since his childhood, Mohammed suffered from many of these identical symptoms. Halabieh, a biographer of Mohammed, mentioned that Mohammed suffered from convulsions since he was one year old. Sahih Al Buchari, in his hadith translations, reported that on one occasion Mohammed fell into a trance while he was a young man before he claimed to have received the Koran. Other Islamic literature, such as Halabieh, states that Mohammed used to go into a coma before he wrote down the Koran, which clearly reveals his direct involvement with Kahaneh. When he started receiving the Koran, he fell

---

[25] Rafat Amari,"Occultism in the Family of Mohammed", *Religion Research Institute*, 2004, http://religionresearchinstitute.org/Mohammad/occultism.htm (accessed February 8, 2011).

into a coma. Anthropologists believe that the priesthood that serves the devil is transmitted from individual to individual in the same family.[26]

Muhammad was probably also influenced by an Ebionite Christian pastor by the name of Waraqa ibn Naufal.

> ..*The Prophet returned to Khadija while his heart was beating rapidly. She (Aisha) took him to Waraqa bin Naufal who was a Christian convert and used to read the Gospel in Arabic. Waraqa asked (the Prophet), "What do you see?" When he told him, Waraqa said, "That is the same angel whom Allah sent to the Prophet Moses. Should I live till you receive the Divine Message, I will support you strongly."*[27]

It must be noted that pastor Naufal was a member of a heretical Judaic Christian sect that only revered Jesus of Nazareth as a great prophet, born of a virgin, performer of

---

[26] Rafat Amari, "Occultism in the Family of Mohammed," *Religion Research Institute*, 2004, http://religionresearchinstitute.org/Mohammad/occultism.htm (accessed February 8, 2011).Much of this information came from *The Book of Idols*, as discussed in Hishām ibn al-Kalbī (Arab scholar):...Collection") as taught by Dr. Rafat Amari at the Religion Research Institute. *The Book of Idols* is a work of great importance about the politics, religion, and literature of the pre-Islamic and early Muslim Arabs.

[27] hadîths narrated in Sahih al-Bukhârî: Narrated 'Aisha[(R)]: Volume 4, Book 55, Number 605:

miracles, and anointed by God to a Gospel that was simply defined as a new interpretation of the law. They taught that salvation came only by means of the law. They did not believe Jesus was divine, crucified, resurrected or the Savior of mankind.[28] The Ebionites were like the Pharisees and opposed Apostle Paul. The early church considered the Ebionites one of the many heretical sects of Christianity. Muhammad spent much time in prayer and fasting in caves in the mountains north of Mecca and probably meditated much on what pastor Naufal taught him.

The Quraysh tribe's most important god was the Moon god called Al-Ilah. Muhammad did not believe in the many gods that were worshipped in the Ka'aba, a place in Mecca which housed many idols and represented many gods. However, Muhammad came to believe that the only true god was Al-Ilah. Al-Ilah, later shortened to *Allah,* was symbolized by the crescent moon. This symbol, which represents Islam to this day, can be found on all mosques throughout the world. For some reason, Muhammad did not see the falsity of worshipping a god who at one time was one of many gods in the Ka'aba.

---

[28] Philip Jenkins, *Hidden Gospels: How the Search for Jesus Lost Its Way* (New York: Oxford University Press, 2001).

It is interesting to note that no one of his time disputed Muhammad's premise that Al-Ilah should be worshipped. They recognized that Al-Ilah (Al-Ilah means "the god") was the moon god, which they took to be the main god of all the gods, but they did not see the necessity of worshipping only him. Even Muhammad, apparently, didn't realize that this belief in Allah did not take into account the nature of God in the abstract, only of the personal position of Allah...the common noun from which Allah is probably derived.

Muhammad was also influenced by the many Star worshippers of his time.[29] These stars or Star Family were worshipped by many in Arabia in the northern part of that country. Venus worship came to be even more important than the moon and sun and soon imposed itself as the monotheistic worship of its time. There are symbols of this Star, Venus, on flags and mosques to this day; it is represented by the crescent moon with a star in the center of it. Venus worship soon took the title of "Allah" from the moon.

---

[29] Rafat Amari, *Islam: In Light of History* (Prospect Heights, IL: Religion Research Institute Publications, 2004), 273-275.

He (Venus) subjected the sun and the moon till they say Allah. Surah 29:61.

Muhammad's first wife, Khadijah, wrote down most of his utterances, which apparently she believed to be the very words of Allah himself. These writings took about 22 years, from 610 to 632 AD. He taught equity, justice, peace and compassion early in his life but later took up the sword to convince his enemies to submit to his truth.

As the years passed, Muhammad came into favor with the Yathrib people in the city of Medina and became a political leader as well as their prophet. It was in Medina that Islam became a religion. As his popularity and followers grew, he made enemies with his old home in Mecca, and wars between the Muslims and Meccans broke out. In time he conquered Mecca, and in 634 AD he gained complete control of Arabia. He died at the age of 64, and it was rumored that he was poisoned.

The following are important dates associated with Muhammad:

- *AD 623 –Muhammad receives a revelation calling for jihad, or holy war, against nonbelievers for the first time. During this year he sends out followers to attack Quraysh caravans, to attack idol* worshipers of Mecca and to attack idol worshipers in Al-Kharrar.

- *AD 624 – Eleven attacks against idol worshippers and raids to obtain wealth.*
- *AD 625 – Muslims defeated in the battle of Uhud. During this year Muhammad had a Jewish leader named Kaab Ibn al-Ashraf assassinated. Also during this year sent out two other raids.*
- *AD 626 – Three raids, one of which was against a Jewish tribe.*
- *AD 627 – Five more raids, one in which he killed all of the men of Beni Qurayzah and took their women and children as captives. Assassinated another Jewish leader, Abi-Rafa.*
- *AD 628 – A few raids.*
- *AD 629 – Five raids and attacked a Jewish village.*
- *AD 630 – Three raids, two battles and the invasion and conquest of Mecca.*
- *AD 631 – This year people from all over the area who Muhammad did not attack sent messengers to him and said they would submit to him. There were forty-eight different groups who submitted. This year he raided Ta-buk.*
- *AD 632 – Sent governors to rule over the areas which submitted to his rule and prophethood.* [30]

---

[30] Mark Gabriel, *Jesus and Muhammad – Profound Difference and Surprising Similarities* (Lake Mary, FL: Frontline – A Strang Company, 2004), 70-73.

As we have seen, the beginnings of Islam can not be traced back earlier than 570 AD when Muhammad was born. Islam has no accepted Biblical writings to give it credence of any kind, and its founder, Muhammad, does not have any spiritual credentials that would lead one to believe he heard anything from God. Even Muhammad's life, people asked him to perform even one miracle or give one sign that gave proof that he was sent from God, but he couldn't.[31]

The beginnings of Christianity and the beginnings of Islam stand in stark contrast to one another. One is founded upon thousands of years of prophetic Biblical writings, attested to by many witnesses, and confirmed by history. The other one can only trace its history back to 570 AD, it has no one who can attest to its claim of divine authenticity, and history can only record the sad methods used to propagate its premise. In Appendix B I will discuss the sad history of the Crusades in Islam's attempt to further their goals.

One of the most outstanding prowesses of Christianity is its ability to trace its lineage to all of the important Biblical personalities. The strength of Jesus' claims of who he was not only could be realized in his daily

---

[31] Surah. 17:90-99.

living, it could be confirmed by what he fulfilled that Scripture demanded that Adam's son would do. The one thing that stood out to those who witnessed Jesus' life was his ability to complete the miracles that could only be attributed to the Messiah.

CHAPTER 3

GOD'S NATURE

In the New Testament, we are told that God is love[1] and that we must love others as He loves them. This powerful pronunciation of God isn't just a religious way of proclaiming an attribute of God, but it describes exactly how God has His being. His being is love; what He does manifests itself in a way that shows mankind what makes Him tick, if you will. Love isn't something God has to work at, He just loves. Humans have to learn to love, but God is love. Everything He does, thinks, and personifies is love, which is His perfection in action.

When we study anything about God or any claim by any religion about God, there should be things we can see that give evidence that what the religion touts is of the true God. If love is the basis of what is proclaimed by any religion, we should see that love manifesting itself and mimicking the god who is proclaimed.

---

[1] 1 Jn. 4:8, 16.

Christianity's God (the God of Abraham, Isaac, Jacob and the Father of Jesus) proclaims that His worshippers must manifest love to all humans. There is no other proof of Christianity's power and ability to change lives and improve the well being of those who come to God through Christ. The call to love stands out as one thing that other humans can see that would give proof that they were of the one true God and sent by Him.[2] Contrasted with the Christian God is the god of Islam. Islam's god is never associated with love. He may be called merciful, but love is not something the average Muslim strives to see in his relationship with Allah. Usually, what the average Muslim strives to do is to please Allah. This pleasing comes from Muhammad's own relationship with Allah, which was one of master-slave association.[3] This master-slave relationship went way beyond the submission a disciple would give his teacher to one of bondage to authority. There seems to be only a working relationship with those associated to Allah instead of a father figure and son relationship as there is in Christianity.

The submission Muhammad gave Allah is constantly manifested in the Koran and the writings about

---

[2] Jn. 13:35.

[3] Surah. 2:23.

Muhammad. There doesn't seem to be an understanding that the Creator would want a relationship with anyone in general. If love wasn't the motivating factor in a relationship with his creation, then it would be enough to demand allegiance. Muhammad gave that allegiance and "required" it of all those who believed in Allah. This allegiance not only must be directed to Allah, but it must be directed to his prophet also. Surah. 14:80 states, *"He who obeys the Messenger, has obeyed Allah."*

The Koran is full of passages that speak of Allah only loving someone if he or she submitted to him instead of loving him because of his nature.

> *If ye love Allah, follow me; Allah will love and forgive you your sins.*
>
> Surah 3:34

> *Allah loves not transgressors.*
>
> Surah 2:190

> *He loves not creatures ungrateful or wicked.*
>
> Surah 2:276

> *Allah loves not those who do wrong.*
>
> Surah 3:57

> *Allah loves not the arrogant, the vainglorious.*
>
> Surah 4:36

But in contrast to Muhammad, Jesus did everything He could to show God through love. Instead of blind obedience as Muhammad gave to Allah, Jesus obeyed because of His love for God the Father.[4] During temptation and suffering, Jesus cried out to Abba (Daddy), Father; which showed His great love and endearment to God.

Jesus' love of the Father was reflected in His relationship with others. In one form or another, Jesus told His disciples that God loved them and wanted the best for them; He made a point to show His disciples that He too loved them and would even die for them.[5] Even to those who were accused of sin, Jesus demonstrated love in order for them to see the truth.[6] He had compassion and refused to have anything bad happen to those who did not accept His message. When His own disciples wanted to bring destruction upon a village, Jesus' love prevented them from pronouncing a curse.

> *And it came to pass, when the time was come that he should be received up, he stedfastly set his face to go to Jerusalem, And sent messengers before his face: and they went, and entered into a village of the*

---

[4] Jn. 14:31.

[5] Jn. 15:9.

[6] Lk. 7:36-50.

Samaritans, to make ready for him. And they did not receive him, because his face was as though he would go to Jerusalem. And when his disciples James and John saw this, they said, Lord, wilt thou that we command fire to come down from heaven, and consume them, even as Elias did? But he turned, and rebuked them, and said, Ye know not what manner of spirit ye are of. For the Son of man is not come to destroy men's lives, but to save them. And they went to another village.

Luke 9:51-56

Contrast this with Muhammad's stance on those who would not accept his message.

And whoever contradicts and opposes the Messenger (Muhammad) after the right path has been shown clearly to him, and follows other than the believers' way, We shall keep him in the path he has chosen, and burn him in Hell-what an evil destination!

Surah 4:115.

Mark A. Gabriel has a diagram that depicts the contrasting differences between Allah and God and the relationship each has with those who believe. This diagram (I have added some items) really makes the point between God's nature as a loving and kind Father and Allah's nature, which is one of demanding and dictatorial overseer.

53

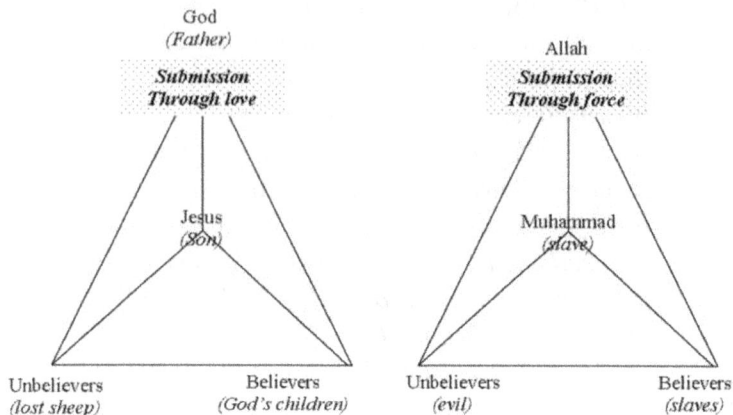

God *(Father)* **Submission Through love** Jesus *(Son)*	Allah **Submission Through force** Muhammad *(slave)*
Unbelievers Believers *(lost sheep)* *(God's children)*	Unbelievers Believers *(evil)* *(slaves)*

One requires submission through love and the other submission by force. [7]

Jesus taught to instill in His disciples that love gave proof of God's approval of those who were considered of Him. It must have been a shock to a people who considered an eye for eye the most proper way of dealing with a wrong done to them.

> *But I say unto you, Love your enemies, bless them that curse you, do good to them that hate you, and pray for them which despitefully use you, persecute you; That ye may be the children of your Father which is in heaven: for he maketh his sun to rise on the evil and on the good, and sendeth rain on the just and on the unjust. For if ye love*

[7] Mark A. Gabriel, *Jesus and Muhammad – Profound Difference and Surprising Similarities* (Lake Mary, FL: Frontline – A Strang Company, 2004), 145.

them which love you, what reward have ye?
Do not even the publicans the same?
Matthew 5:44-46

One can not escape the nature of God as one studies the Bible; His nature permeates every book, most events, and touches each person who has any dealings with Him. It was, and is, as if God has done and will do anything to make us see Him for who He is – Love. Love is the fragrance, the photograph, and very essence of all one would consider good. It depicts God and rules out any vindictiveness or arbitrary indifference.

The nature of God flows from His being and touches His son, Jesus. His son speaks to us through Scripture and guides us along life's roads, encounters, and peoples we come in contact with. His instructions call from the centuries of time and speak to us to consider others first and never to do anything from selfish motives. Christ's teaching touches everything in life and does not give us permission to lessen in our demonstration of the One we believe in. From the love towards God to the love towards our enemies, to women, children, and slave there is no denying which path God's disciples must take.

The Christian faith and the Islam religion have a total opposite approach to love and how one would love others. The following analogies are found in each of the two religion's writings:

Women

Islam teaches that women are the property of man. Love does not seem to play a role in their relationship nor does mutual respect come into play as man is the head, final word and sovereign in a marriage.

- Women are inferior to men – Surah 4:38
- Women are likened to a field (tilth) – Surah 2:223
- Women's testimony is only half of a man's – Surah 2:282
- Girls who have not yet menstruated can be taken as a wife – Surah 65:4 (Muhammad married Aisha when she was six years old and consummated the marriage when she was nine years old.)
- Muhammad basically said that women were evil and even much more so than men.[8]
- Wives can be beaten if they do not submit to their husband's sexual advances.[9]

---

[8] Mark Gabriel, *Jesus and Muhammad – Profound Difference and Surprising Similarities* (Lake Mary, FL: Frontline – A Strang Company, 2004), 91-92.

[9] Sahih al-Bukhari *(the Correct books of Bukhar). Volume 7, Book 62, Number 121:* English translation by Dr. Muhammad Mushasin Khan., http://www.usc.edu/schools/college/crcc/engagement/resources/texts/m

The Hadith teaches: (Hadithes were the collection of sayings and actions of Muhammad that his followers gradually collected and kept in many volumes. They came to have as much authority as the Koran.) [10]

- *Women are inferior to men in mental capacity.* [11]
- *Women walking in front of a man praying annuls his prayers.* [12]

The Prophet said: "I was shown the Hell-fire and that the majority of its dwellers were women who were ungrateful." It was asked, "Do they disbelieve in Allah?" (or are they ungrateful to Allah?) He replied, "They are ungrateful to their husbands and are ungrateful for the favors and the good (charitable deeds) done to them. If you have always been good (benevolent) to one of them and then she sees something in you (not of her liking), she will say, 'I have never received any good from you.'"

---

uslim/hadith/bukhari/009.sbt.html (accessed May 3, 2010), Accessed at University of Southern California web site.

[10] The two Hadith collections regarded as the most accurate are those by Al-Bukari and Sayyid Muslim.

[11] Hadith 1:301.

[12] Sahih al-Bukhari *(the Correct books of Bukhar). Volume 1, Book 9, Number 490:* English translation by Dr. Muhammad Mushasin Khan.,
http://www.usc.edu/schools/college/crcc/engagement/resources/texts/m uslim/hadith/bukhari/009.sbt.html (accessed May 3, 2010), Accessed at University of Southern California web site.

Narrated Ibn 'Abbas: *Volume 1, Book 2, Number 28:*

The things which annul the prayers were mentioned before me. They said, "Prayer is annulled by a dog, a donkey and a woman (if they pass in front of the praying people)." I said, "You have made us (i.e. women) dogs." I saw the Prophet praying while I used to lie in my bed between him and the Qibla. Whenever I was in need of something, I would slip away. For I disliked to face him.

Narrated 'Aisha: *Volume 1, Book 9, Number 490:*

Once Allah's Apostle went out to the Musalla (to offer the prayer) o 'Id-al-Adha or Al-Fitr prayer. Then he passed by the women and said, "O women! Give alms, as I have seen that the majority of the dwellers of Hell-fire were you (women)." They asked, "Why is it so, O Allah's Apostle?" He replied, "You curse frequently and are ungrateful to your husbands. I have not seen anyone more deficient in intelligence and religion than you. A cautious sensible man could be led astray by some of you." The women asked, "O Allah's Apostle! What is deficient in our intelligence and religion?" He said, "Is not the evidence of two women equal to the witness of one man?" They replied in the affirmative. He said, "This is the deficiency in her intelligence. Isn't it true that a woman can neither pray nor fast during her menses?" The women replied in the affirmative. He said, "This is the deficiency in her religion."

Narrated Abu Said Al-Khudri: *Vol. 1, Book 6,*
Number 301:

Christianity teaches that women are co-equal with men, but men have a greater responsibility to them. Love plays a great role in the marriage relationship, and when love is displayed, the wife would respond in kind. The Bible teaches:

> *Husbands, love your wives, even as Christ also loved the church, and gave himself for it; That he might sanctify and cleanse it with the washing of water by the word, That he might present it to himself a glorious church, not having spot, or wrinkle, or any such thing; but that it should be holy and without blemish. So ought men to love their wives as their own bodies. He that loveth his wife loveth himself. For no man ever yet hated his own flesh; but nourisheth and cherisheth it, even as the Lord the church: For we are members of his body, of his flesh, and of his bones. For this cause shall a man leave his father and mother, and shall be joined unto his wife, and they two shall be one flesh. This is a great mystery: but I speak concerning Christ and the church. Nevertheless let every one of you in particular so love his wife even as himself; and the wife see that she reverence her husband.*
>
> Ephesians 5:25-33

Likewise, ye husbands, dwell with them according to knowledge, giving honour unto

*the wife, as unto the weaker vessel, and as
being heirs together of the grace of life; that
your prayers be not hindered.*

1 Peter 3:7

Christian teaching stands in stark contrast to Islamic
teaching in that Christianity accepts
women as co-laborers with men and
directs men to not only love their wives
but to walk with them in an equal

> *Husbands
> love your
> wives!*

understanding of grace and life purpose. The husband is to
recognize the woman's physical and probably emotional
makeup as weaker, but not to see her as spiritually less then
himself. Both of their prayers depend on unity and a
flowing of mutual respect and love.

This approach to male and female love comes from
a direct relational understanding of God's love towards all
of mankind as taught through the Bible and Christian
teaching.

<u>Enemies</u>

Islam teaches that anyone who does not accept the
beliefs of Allah or turns away from Islam is an enemy of
Allah and must be dealt with in the gravest of ways. M. Ali,
a former Muslim, in his book, *Islam Reviewed,* makes the
assertion that those who carry out Jihad *(Striving. Fighting
against one's own sinful self. Also, a physical fight for the*

truth of Islam against those who oppose Islam, or "Holy War.") are the true Muslims because the Koran declares it so.[13]

> *Therefore when ye meet the unbelievers smite at their necks; at length, when ye have thoroughly subdued them, bind a bond firmly on them.*
>
> Surah 47:4

> *The blood of a Muslim who confesses that none has the right to be worshipped but Allah and that I am His Apostle, cannot be shed except in three cases: In Qisas for murder, a married person who commits illegal sexual intercourse and the one who reverts from Islam (apostate) and leaves the Muslims.*
>
> Sahih Bukari, Volume 9, Book 83, Number 17

The nature of Allah is revealed in his stance towards those who strive against his enemies. (Remember, anyone who does not accept Islam or Islam's prophet is considered an enemy.) It seems to matter more to Allah that his followers fight for him as opposed to those who are his as a matter of heart.

> *Allah has preferred in grades those who strive hard and fight with their wealth and*

---

[13] M. Ali, *Islam Reviewed* (Fort Myers, FL: Fish House Publishing, 1999), 89.

their lives above those who sit. Unto each,
Allah has promised good, but Allah has
preferred those who strive hard and fight,
above those who sit by a huge reward.

Surah 4:95

A main enemy of Islam and Muslims is the Jew.
There has been no love loss on the part of Allah toward the
other son of Abraham, Isaac. Even though Muslims believe
that Abraham is the patriarch of their linage, they refuse to
accept Isaac or the Jews as their fellow sojourners on this
planet.

Muhammad taught that the Jews were the source of
many evils and conflicts in the world. The Jews were to be
eliminated wherever they were found. Muhammad believed
this because he claimed that this hatred came from Allah
towards all Jews.

O, true believer, take not the Jews and
Christians for your friends. They cannot be
trusted. They are defiled...filth.

Surah 5:51

Wherever they are found, the Jew reeks of
destruction – which is their just reward.

Surah 3:112

The Jews are smitten with vileness and
misery and drew on themselves indignation
from Allah.

Surah 2:61

It seems that Allah's hatred for the Jews is so strong that he will not permit the Muslims to be resurrected until all the Jews on the earth have been completely destroyed. Dr. James Murk in his book, *"Islam Rising – The Never Ending Jihad Against The Jews and Israel,"* describes this hatred of Allah towards the Jews is realized in "three no's"; *"no peace, no negotiations, and no recognition."* [14]

> *The Hour (day of resurrection) will not arrive until the Muslims make war against the Jews and kill them, and until a Jew will hide behind a rock or tree, and the rock and the tree will say: "Oh Muslim, a servant of Allah, there is a Jew behind me, come and kill him."*
> Hadith of Sahih al-Bukhari
> 2922

> *"Therefore when ye meet the unbelievers smite at their necks; at length, when ye have thoroughly subdued them, bind a bond firmly on them."*

Even in the modern times the heart of Allah towards the Jews seems to permeate much of the thought of those who give him allegiance. James Murk has cataloged many statements by leading Islamic scholars and political leaders of our time. The statements of hate do not seem to be the

[14] Jim Murk, *Islam Rising - The Never Ending Jihad Against The Jew and Israel,* Book Two (Springfield, MO: 21st Century Press, 2007), 29.

exception to the rule, but the norm. [15] Statements to entirely eliminate the Jews from the face of the earth and to finish what Hitler tried to do did not stand out as fanatical but a normative way of portraying what Allah would have Muslims do to the object of his hatred, the Jew.

Christianity teaches what matters to the true God is mercy, and it isn't a matter of fighting, it is a matter of knowing God's heart and compassion towards anyone who doesn't understand. Constantly, we see in the Bible God's heart being revealed towards everyone, the enemies of God and the friends of God alike.

> *Even so have these also now not believed, that through your mercy they also may obtain mercy. For God hath concluded them all in unbelief, that he might have mercy upon all.*
>
> Romans 11:31-32

Christianity teaches that the Jew is the Apple of God's eye and favored by Him as those to whom He chose to reveal Himself. The Jew holds a special place in God's heart and He will fulfill His promise made to Abraham and all of his descendants to and through Jesus.

> *I speak the truth in Christ — I am not lying, my conscience confirms it in the Holy Spirit— I have great sorrow and unceasing*

---

[15] Ibid., 102-107.

anguish in my heart. For I could wish that I myself were cursed and cut off from Christ for the sake of my brothers, those of my own race, the people of Israel. Theirs is the adoption as sons; theirs the divine glory, the covenants, the receiving of the law, the temple worship and the promises. Theirs are the patriarchs, and from them is traced the human ancestry of Christ, who is God over all, forever praised! Amen.

Romans 9:1-5

But you, O Israel, my servant, Jacob, whom I have chosen, you descendants of Abraham my friend, I took you from the ends of the earth, from its farthest corners I called you. I said, "You are my servant"; I have chosen you and have not rejected you. So do not fear, for I am with you; do not be dismayed, for I am your God. I will strengthen you and help you; I will uphold you with my righteous right hand. "All who rage against you will surely be ashamed and disgraced; those who oppose you will be as nothing and perish. Though you search for your enemies, you will not find them. Those who wage war against you will be as nothing at all. For I am the Lord, your God, who takes hold of your right hand and says to you, Do not fear; I will help you. 14 Do not be afraid, O worm Jacob, O little Israel, for I myself will help you," declares the Lord, your Redeemer, the Holy One of Israel.

Isaiah 41:8-14

It seems to stand out that the Jew – Israel has a special place in God's eternal plan for mankind. Even though in the twenty-first century the only mention of Israel is within the contexts of conflict there can't be any biblical proof that God has abandoned nor will He abandon the Jew. God will bless those who bless Israel and will curse those who curse her!

There are many scriptural promises that speak of God bringing the Jew back to her ancient land and blessing him/her. Far from seeing Israel as a pig or monkey as the Koran depicts her,[16] God see her as a special protected child that He will bless and prosper. Although Israel may have wandered from her special place in God's plan, He has not abandoned her; rather He will bring about His promise for her.

---

[16] Surah 7:166, Surah 5:60, Surah 2:65.

CHAPTER 4

GOD PERMITS US TO KNOW HIM

Then the word of the Lord came to me: "This is what the Lord, the God of Israel, says: 'Like these good figs, I regard as good the exiles from Judah, whom I sent away from this place to the land of the Babylonians. My eyes will watch over them for their good, and I will bring them back to this land. I will build them up and not tear them down; I will plant them and not uproot them. I will give them a heart to know me, that I am the Lord. They will be my people, and I will be their God, for they will return to me with all their heart.'"

Jeremiah 24:4-7

And this is life eternal, that they might know thee the only true God, and Jesus Christ, whom thou hast sent.

John 17:3

One of the most outstanding acknowledgements about God that we see in the Hebraic and Christian beliefs is His desire for mankind to know Him. God goes out of

67

His way in order for His creation to know Him, comprehend (at least in part) and to become one with Him. We may call it a mystery that God would want us to know Him since He is so beyond man's make up and power. Yet God calls out to us to come, abide, tarry, wait, sojourn, rest, and walk with Him; all of these verbs call us to an action with its center to focus upon God. He wants us to know Him!

Imagine, if you will, a being that is the only power there is; the mind to know all things, create all things, is the only one of his kind there is and would want his creation to know him for who he is. This is the heart of God; this is the person of God through whom we have our life. This Creator wants you and me to know!

Our Creator goes to great lengths to reveal Himself to us. First, He calls Himself Father. Father! We get a piercing look into the mind and heart of our creator and see the tender makeup of a being we could never understand with our finite minds. Yet He opens to us what His greatest desire is. He desires children who know Him. He desires an intercourse of life and a free flowing of mutual love.

> *Doubtless thou art our father, though Abraham be ignorant of us, and Israel acknowledge us not: thou, O Lord, art our*

*father, our redeemer; thy name is from
everlasting.   Isaiah 63:16
But now, O Lord, thou art our father; we are
the clay, and thou our potter; and we all are
the work of thy hand.*
Isaiah 64:8

*Wherefore come out from among them, and
be ye separate, saith the Lord, and touch not
the unclean thing; and I will receive you,
And will be a Father unto you, and ye shall
be my sons and daughters, saith the Lord
Almighty.*
2 Corinthians 6:17-18

*One God and Father of all, who is above all,
and through all, and in you all.*
Ephesians 4:6

In the New Testament, God is called "Father" 245 times.
There is nothing impersonal or aloof with the God of the
Bible; He takes the risk in letting us know Him and even
restricts Himself as to our responses to Him and how we
reflect our relationship with what He does for us. He makes
Himself vulnerable to our love or lack thereof, but in no
case does He force us to know Him. John Sanders, in his
great book, *The God Who Risks,* explains it this way:

> *...God is the perfection of love and
> communion – the very antithesis of
> aloofness, isolation and domination. God is
> no solitary potentate forcing his will on
> others. ...Personhood, relational and*

69

community – not power, independence and control – become the center for understanding the nature of God. ...A God who is antecedently relational and self-sufficient is free to create significant others and enter into genuine reciprocal relations with them. [1]

The concept that God would want us to know Him in a very personal way is difficult for many to accept. It flies in the face of religions that see God as impersonal, aloof or dictatorial. Their acceptance of a god who would listen to our cries, respond to our love and welcome our input is too much to absorb. Their response to this is to retreat into legalism and/or make-believe. To many, God can't be lowered to our understanding of personal relationship or reciprocal communion that allows for each being to know the other. From these ways of thinking come false religions that can only see God as a force that must be reckoned with instead of a being who wants us to know Him and share His life.

This personal God, if we will see Him as wanting a personal relationship with us, doesn't leave us to ourselves to know Him personally, He went to great lengths to reveal Himself in order that we may know. He sent His Son,

[1] John Sanders, *The God Who Risks*, Second Edition (Downers Grove, IL: IVP Academic, 2007), 177-178.

Jesus, to Earth, who was a man like us. He taught and lived among us to show us the Father, and then after His mission of love in death and resurrection, He made it possible for us to know the Father by living in us. This, then, is the greatest differences of all religions; Christianity teaches that the true God can live in humans.

Tim Stafford, in his book *Knowing the Face of God –The Search of a Personal Relationship with God,* shares that the only true way a person can know someone else is by spending time with them in all aspects of their lives. [2] But the only true way we know or have a personal relationship is from within. We know ourselves from within, not from without, and that same reality stands true when it comes to God, the only way we can really know God is by Him living within us.

Stafford's concept of a true relationship with God is really the very foundation of the Christian principle of a relationship. Every person must come to that realization or he or she falls short in the quest for true relationship with God.

> *Jesus answered and said unto him, If a man love me, he will keep my words: and my*

[2] Tim Stafford, *Knowing the Face of God – The Search for a Personal Relationship with God* (Grand Rapids, MI: Zondervan Publishing House, 1986).

Father will love him, and we will come unto him, and make our abode with him.

John 14:23

The Hebraic and Christian Biblical concept of God does not give room for guessing or surmising; it precisely declares what God wants and who is the object of His desires. God created out of love so that He could share Himself with those He created and that they would know Him intimately

> *And this is life eternal, that they might know thee the only true God, and Jesus Christ, whom thou hast sent.*
>
> John 17:3

> *But now, O Lord, thou art our father; we are the clay, and thou our potter; and we all are the work of thy hand.*
>
> Isaiah 64:8

Islam's God is not personal.

Islamic teaching does not even consider that God would want us to know Him, much less know Him as a father. It is even considered to be blasphemous to say, *"I am a child of God."*

> *And (both) the Jews and the Christians say: "We are the children of Allah and His love ones." Say: "Why then does He punish you for your sins?" Nay, you are but human beings of those He has created...*

Surah 5:18

There are ninety nine names for god in the Koran.
When you read the whole Koran, from the first to the last
surah, you will not find the word "father" or "love"
attributed to God. God is not father in Islam. God is not
love in Islam. But in Christianity we find both father and
love depicted of God.

Dr. Labib Mikhail, says this about the god of Islam:

*When the disciples came to Jesus and they
told Him, "Teach us to pray?" What did He
say? "When you pray you say, 'Our father
who art in heaven...'" But in Islam god,
Allah, is no father. Why did Islam deny the
fatherhood of God? Because if Islam would
confess the fatherhood of God, it demands
that they will confess that eternal sonship of
Jesus Christ, because there is no eternal
fatherhood without eternal sonship. This is
why, when you read the Quran, God is no
father. If he is a father, and this is one of his
attributes, he must have a son. And of
course, He is a father for eternity, then the
son should be eternal also, or else there will
not be any eternal fatherhood. That is one
thing that we have to consider in the
attributes of God, the difference in the
attributes of God between Islam and
Christianity.* [3]

[3] Labib Mikhail, *Is Allah of Muslims the God of Christians?*,
http://www.thespiritofislam.com/god-allah/45-would-you-elaborate-on-that-very-first-point.html (accessed February 9, 2011).

73

Even though the Koran has ninety nine descriptive names for Allah, those names seem to reflect his nature only for and towards those who submit instead of his normal loving makeup. Submission from Allah's creation is more important than a personal loving relationship with his creation. Apparently, Allah does not want mankind to know him, but just to obey him.

CHAPTER 5

WHO IS GOD

Hebraic, Christian and Islamic Scripture have distinctions in the way each sees God's eternal makeup, but as a whole each accepts that God is a monotheistic God.

Most of Christian believers accept the fact that God is revealed through a trinity (a better word to use would be "tri-unity") made up of Father, Son and Holy Spirit. This is not to say that there are three Gods who work together, but a tri-unity of one being that operates in one essence. J. Hampton Keathley teaches it in the following way:

> **Essence:** *In its theological usage, essence refers to "the intrinsic or indispensable, permanent, and inseparable qualities that characterize or identify the being of God." The words tri-unity and trinity are used to refer to the fact that the Bible speaks of one God, but attributes the characteristics of God to three Persons: Father, Son, and Holy Spirit. The doctrine of the trinity states that there is one God who is one in essence or substance, but three in personality. This*

does not mean three independent Gods existing as one, but three Persons who are co-equal, co-eternal, inseparable, interdependent, and eternally united in one absolute Divine Essence and Being.[1]

Austin De Bourg makes it a point that Christians must teach and emphasize that God exists alone and that there cannot be another God.[2]

Judaism does not accept the tri-unity of God. In Judaism, the idea of God as a duality or trinity is heretical — it's even considered by some polytheistic. According to Judaic beliefs, the Torah rules out a trinitarian God in Deuteronomy (6:4): *"Hear Israel, the Lord is our God, the Lord is one."* The belief that Jesus (or any other human) is God, any deity, the son of God, or a person of the Trinity, is incompatible with traditional Jewish philosophical tenets. The same applies to belief in Jesus as the Messiah or a prophet of God; those beliefs are also contrary to traditional Jewish views. The idea of the Jewish Messiah is different from the Christian Christ because Jews believe Jesus did not fulfill Jewish Messianic prophecies that establish the

---

[1] J. Hampton Keathley, "The Tinity (Triunity) of God," *Bible.org,* May 18, 2004, http://bible.org/article/trinity-triunity-god (accessed January 23/2011).

[2] Austin De Bourg, *Insights into the Mystery of the Trinity* (Enumclaw, WA: WinePress Publishing, 2006), 31.

criteria for the coming of the Messiah. Authoritative texts of Judaism reject Jesus as God, Divine Being, intermediary between humans and God, Messiah or saint. The belief in the Trinity is also held to be incompatible with Judaism as are many other tenets of Christianity.

Islam basically believes the same as Judaism and considers it a blasphemy to even think of God as anything but one eternal being.

> *People of the Book, do not go to excess in your religion, and do not say anything about God except the truth: the Messiah, Jesus, son of Mary, was nothing more than a messenger of God, His word, directed to Mary, a spirit from Him. So believe in God and His messengers and do not speak of a "Trinity"—stop, that is better for you—God is only one God, He is far above having a son, everything in the heavens and earth belongs to Him and He is the best one to trust.*
> Koran 4:171, M. A. S. Abdel-Haleem translation.

> *Those who say, "God is the Messiah, son of Mary," have defied God. The Messiah himself said, "Children of Israel, worship God, my Lord and your Lord." If anyone associates others with God, God will forbid him from the Garden, and Hell will be his home. No one will help such evildoers. Those people who say that God is the third of three are defying [the truth]: there is only One*

God. If they persist in what they are saying, a painful punishment will afflict those of them who persist. Why do they not turn to God and ask his forgiveness, when God is most forgiving, most merciful? The Messiah, son of Mary, was only a messenger; other messengers had come and gone before him; his mother was a virtuous woman; both ate food. See how clear we make these signs for them; see how deluded they are."

Koran 5:72 onwards, M. A. S. Abdel-Haleem – translation

When God says, "Jesus, son of Mary, did you say to people, 'Take me and my mother as two gods alongside God?' he will say, 'May You be exalted! I would never say what I had no right to say—if I had said such a thing You would have known it: You know all that is within me, though I do not know what is within You, You alone have full knowledge of things unseen."

Surah 5:116, M. A. S. Abdel-Haleem translation

Each of these major religions depicts God and His relationship to man in totally different ways. Christianity looks to God to physically return to Earth as the Son, Jesus the Messiah. Judaism looks for the messiah of God to come from the earth, born of human parents and directing the will of God, but not God Himself. Islam looks for the Mahdi who will be a descendent of Muhammad and will be human.[3]

[3] See Appendix A.

CHAPTER 6

DOES GOD HAVE A SON?

One of the great topics of most religions is the topic whether God has a son or not. Most religions do not believe that God has a son nor can they accept that God would want a son. They believe God is too far above humans, and they can not even conceive of the thought that He has those qualities that would permit Him to have a son. Judaism, Christianity and Islam all have a monotheistic belief in God. Although Christianity believes God is one, He is a plural being made up of Father, Son, and Holy Spirit.

Judaism:

Most people believe that the concept of God having a Son came from the Christian believers long after the earthly Church was formed. However, the concept and belief in God having a son was in the Tanakh (The Old Testament).

> *Thou art my Son; this day have I begotten thee.*

There are many strong analogies of the son of God in other Jewish writings and especially in the Tanakh. Although many make reference to King David and his offspring, most are a direct promise or decree to one of David's descendants- the Messiah who would come and show mankind the Father.

> *Why do the nations conspire and the peoples plot in vain? The kings of the earth take their stand and the rulers gather together against the Lord and against his Anointed One. "Let us break their chains," they say, "and throw off their fetters." The One enthroned in heaven laughs; the Lord scoffs at them. Then he rebukes them in his anger and terrifies them in his wrath, saying, "I have installed my King on Zion, my holy hill." I will proclaim the decree of the Lord: He said to me, "You are my Son;today I have become your Father. Ask of me, and I will make the nations your inheritance, the ends of the earth your possession. You will rule them with an iron scepter;you will dash them to pieces like pottery." Therefore, you kings, be wise; be warned, you rulers of the earth. Serve the Lord with fear and rejoice with trembling. Kiss the Son, lest he be angry and you be destroyed in your way, for his wrath can flare up in a moment. Blessed are all who take refuge in him.*
>
> Psalm 2:1-12

Christianity:

Christianity's whole premise and foundation rest on the belief that God's Son was born on the earth to set mankind free from the waywardness of man's disobedience to God's will and ways. Jesus, God's Son, was to be the propitiation to God on mankind's behalf. All of this rests on the fact that one must believe that God had or has a son. If the belief in a Son of God is not accepted, then one would not be considered a true Christian.

The New Testament gives many statements of Jesus being God's Son:

Hebrews 1:8: About the Son he says, *"Your throne, O God, will last for ever and ever."*

Colossians 2:9-10: *"In Christ all the fullness of the Deity lives in bodily form."*

Hebrews and Colossians describe Jesus as the exact representation of the divine Father. John's gospel quotes Jesus at length regarding his relationship with his heavenly Father. It also contains two famous attributes of divinity to Jesus.

John 1:1: *"The Word was God"* [in context, the *Word* is Jesus; see Christ the Logos]

John 20:28: *"Thomas said to him, 'My Lord and my God!'"*

There are direct references to Jesus as God found in the following New Testament letters and Gospels.

Romans 9:5: *"Christ, who is God over all"*

Titus 2:13: *"...our great God and Savior, Jesus Christ"*

2 Peter 1:1: *"our God and Savior Jesus Christ"*

Matthew 28:19: *"Go and make disciples of all nations, baptizing them in the name [note the singular] of the Father and of the Son and of the Holy Spirit."*

John 10:25-30: *Jesus answered, "I did tell you, but you do not believe. The miracles I do in my Father's name speak for me, but you do not believe because you are not my sheep. My sheep listen to my voice; I know them, and they follow me. I give them eternal life, and they shall never perish; no one can snatch them out of my hand. My Father, who has given them to me, is greater than all; no one can snatch them out of my Father's hand.I and the Father are one."*

Islam:

Islam totally denies that God has a son and considers it a blasphemy to even speak of such a reality. Islam rejects that Jesus was God incarnate or God the Son, stating that he was a man who, like other prophets, had been divinely chosen to spread God's message. Islamic texts forbid the association of partners with God, emphasizing the notion of God's divine oneness. Numerous titles are given to Jesus in the Koran, such as al-Masīḥ ("the messiah; the anointed one" i.e. by means of blessings), although it does not correspond with the meaning accrued in Christian belief. Jesus is seen in Islam as a precursor to Muhammad. In Islam, Jesus is a messenger of God who had been sent to guide the Children of Israel with a new Scripture, the gospel. The Koran, believed by Muslims to be God's final revelation, states that Jesus was born to Mary (Arabic: Maryam) as the result of virginal conception, a miraculous event that occurred by the decree of God. To aid him in his quest, Jesus was given the ability to perform miracles, all by the permission of God. According to Islamic texts, Jesus was neither killed nor crucified, but rather he was raised alive up to heaven. Islamic traditions narrate that he will return to earth near the Day of Judgment to restore justice and defeat al-Masīḥ ad-Dajjāl (lit. "The false messiah," also known as the Antichrist). Although Jesus is a highly respected prophet in Islam and considered to be the Messiah, Muslims do not believe that he was the son of God. Muslims consider Jesus, the son of the virgin Mary, as a great prophet and the same as other prophets: Noah, Abraham, Moses, Muhammad. Muslims believe that associating others with God in any kind of worship is polytheism, an unforgiveable sin, even if the associated person is an angel or prophet.

Since Christianity, Judaism, and Islam all have their beliefs and sacred text about Jesus, it is obviously futile to believe any of them unless there would be some proof as to what they teach. Was there a person who claimed to be God's Son, and did He give evidence to that fact? In chapter two I discussed the beginnings of Christianity and Islam and gave ample evidence of Jesus' claim to be God's Son and, therefore, will not reiterate those facts again.

The final proof if God had or has a Son will come in the fullness of time. This book and research can neither prove nor deny the claims of Jesus' Sonship. Many throughout the world profess to a dramatic encounter with God's Son. The proof to those people is in their new found lives that were changed when they acknowledged Jesus as Savior and God's Son. Their testimonies are too numerous to add to this book but can be found in any book store or on any web site that speaks of encounters with Jesus.

CHAPTER 7

WHAT FORM OF WORSHIP DOES GOD REQUIRE?

Yet a time is coming and has now come when the true worshipers will worship the Father in spirit and truth, for they are the kind of worshipers the Father seeks. God is spirit, and his worshipers must worship in spirit and in truth.

John 4:23

When we study the different forms of worship that religions around the earth practice, we find similarities both in thought and action, but for the most part, they all have one thing in common. The common thread that flows in all of the religions of the world is the thread of rituals and prayer. Rituals come from some understanding of the deity that is worshipped and its demands of approachability by those who give their allegiance to it. The prayers given to the deity worshipped usually come from some ancestral history that was passed down year after year, and often the reason for them has been lost over time. Both of these, prayers and rituals, usually stand as foundational footing to continue worshipping the deity who is accepted as God or a god. Christianity, Judaism, and Islam are no different than any other form of religion, and they have their rituals and prayers as well.

We are admonished in the Christian Scripture to be led by God in our worship of Him and not to conform to any worldly ways as we approach Him. We are told to make sure our thinking is transformed by spiritual discernment and not worldly discernment alone.

> *Therefore, I urge you, brothers, in view of God's mercy, to offer your bodies as living sacrifices, holy and pleasing to God — this is your spiritual act of worship. Do not conform any longer to the pattern of this world, but be transformed by the renewing of your mind. Then you will be able to test and approve what God's will is — his good, pleasing and perfect will.*
>
> Romans 12:1-2

It does matter to God how we approach Him and how we worship Him. It stands to reason that a supreme being, holy and without blemish, creator of everything would demand that His creation approach Him with respect and awe and not make light of His personage. If there is only one God, and this student believes there is, then it is very important that we know Him, worship Him and address Him as He deserves. We must not make Him out to be something He is not, nor should we surmise as to His being in general. It would make sense that if the one true God demands that we approach Him properly, He would make sure He told us who He is and what He requires of us.

Christianity declares that the one true God has told mankind who He is and what is required of us. In Chapter 2, *Beginnings,* I discussed how we obtained the sacred Scriptures of the Christian, Jewish, and Islamic faiths. Those Scriptures give references to how God/god would want His/his worshippers to approach and adore Him/him. Obviously, the adherence of these religions would follow some type of authoritative documentation, and the authoritative documents ends up being either the Bible or the Koran. Judaism accepts the first five books of the Bible, or the Torah, as authoritative, which is also accepted by Christians who accept the entire Old Testament as well as the New Testament. Muslims accept the Koran as well as the Hadiths.[1] These Scriptures have then become the script, if you will, whereby each religion finds its form of worship and the acceptable style that their God/god requires of them.

---

[1] A *hadith* is a saying of Muhammad or a report about something he did and recorded by his close followers and leaders.

CHRISTIANITY

Christians believe that the form of worship God requires of them is from a free heart, totally dedicated to God, but one which is in spirit and truth.[2] In spirit comes from the Greek word *"pneuma* – πνεῦμα*,"* and in these contexts means a rational soul or a right mental disposition. In other words, it is important to God that we worship Him from our soul, as well as our body and spirit. Our soul, which is our mental and emotional makeup, must be touched by the truth of God's word and His spirit, or we would not be able to approach Him in worship properly.

The proper form of worship, then, for the Christian is one that has his mental as well as his spiritual thinking in order. The order that God requires comes from His call for us to love Him with our whole being; nothing can be left out, it has to be total.

> *Love the Lord your God with all your heart and with all your soul and with all your strength.*
>
> Deut 6:5

> *Jesus replied: "Love the Lord your God with all your heart and with all your soul and with all your mind. This is the first and greatest commandment. And the second is like it: 'Love your neighbor as yourself.' All*

---

[2] John 4:23.

the Law and the Prophets hang on these two commandments."

Matt 22:37-40

Pray without ceasing!

Jesus often told His disciples that what we do and how we worship does make a difference to God. Our worship can not be from rote or doing it just to be doing it, it must come from the heart and be free of those things that would speak of pride when finished. Love must be at the very center of worship, completely unfettered of bondage and totally free from fear or retribution.

Christian worship may have rituals that are man made, but they do not take the place of an open heart towards God and an honest adherence to His will. The adherence to His will comes from a relationship that is founded through the sacrifice of God's Son and not any other sacrifice that man would try to manufacture. Biblical

Rituals do not take the place of an open heart towards God!

Christianity does not give room for repetitive rituals that mean nothing to God, nor does it truthfully demand these rituals for salvation or a right standing with God.

91

Through the centuries, Christianity has been plagued with denominations that try to force rituals upon the believer, but in the long run these have given way to those who desire a free and open form of worship that comes from the heart.

Christianity has its days of remembrance, holy holidays, and sacraments, but these are not usually taught to ensure one's eternity, but only to remind us of a proper way to live and to remember God's grace towards mankind.

Baptism[3] and the Lord's Supper (Communion)[4] are two sacraments that most Christian denominations have in common, but most do not require their practice for someone to be right with God. However, even if a denomination within Christianity requires these two sacraments, they would give room for someone who could not partake of them at a certain moment or an ongoing

---

[3] This represents being born again after burial of old self through a repentant heart and surrender to God's will.

4 When Jesus had the last supper, he took some bread, broke it and shared it with the disciples. He passed a big cup of wine around the group. He told them that he must die to save mankind, and they must always share the bread and wine in remembrance of him. Ever since then Christians have held services called Holy Communion or the Lord's Supper where they have shared blessed bread and wine and given thanks for Jesus' life, death and resurrection.

frequency. What would be more important to these denominations would be the heart attitude of the believer.

Christianity teaches that in all things with God it is very important not to be repetitive in our worship of God. Doing things over and over again does not constitute to God true worship; prayer, celebration and daily living must all be performed because one is in love with God and truly desires to be one with Him instead of only submissive to Him.

Prayer is an avenue of true worship. Prayer in Christianity is taught as a dialogue with God and not just a form of ritual. Prayer becomes a communing with God, an intercourse of love and thought as well as a reminder of one's surrender, allegiance and focus.

> *But when you pray, go into your room, close the door and pray to your Father, who is unseen. Then your Father, who sees what is done in secret, will reward you. And when you pray, do not keep on babbling like pagans, for they think they will be heard because of their many words. Do not be like them, for your Father knows what you need before you ask him.*
> Matt 6:6-8

Here again we see the all important concept of God as Father, God's desire to dialogue with us as His children instead of just His creation. Prayer then comes to be a living part of one's life as would be between an earthly father and his child. It can't be emphasized enough that Christianity almost demands relationship with God, and works of prayer or any other form of works without an intimate and relational life with God does not please Him.

Jesus' example of intimate and daily prayer with His Father taught His disciples to seek, listen to, and follow up with God's desires. He went as far as to say that He (Jesus) would do nothing but only what His Father told Him.[5] He said that He knew that His Father heard Him. [6]

The form of prayer is not necessarily important in the Christian faith as it is in other religions. How one would pray is not important; kneeling, standing, totally prostate, or sitting is not important to Christianity, but what is in the heart is.

This, then, is one of those things that separate Christianity from other religions; it teaches and believes that God hears the one who prays, and if he prays in the name of His Son Jesus, God will give him what he asks.[7] This stands in stark contrast to religions that believe that

---

[5] John 8:29.

[6] John 14:24, 11:41-42.

[7] John 15:16.

prayer is a constant mixture of words that "try" to get their deity's attention and hopefully he will answer.

ISLAM

The Koran does not teach the fatherhood or personal aspect of God and for that reason worship in Islam takes on a much different approach than does Christianity.

Although the Koran provides for the following information, much of it can be found in Emory C. Bogle's book *Islam – Origin & Belief.*

Islam's worship takes on more of a dictatorial approach, and it is mandatory for each of its believers to adhere to its Five Pillars of faith. The Five Pillars of faith are (1) Profess their faith *(shahadah)* at all times; (2) Perform five daily prayers *(salat)*; (3) Annually contribute alms *(zakat)*; (4) Annually perform a thirty-day fast *(siyam)*; and (5) Make at least one pilgrimage *(hajj)* to Mecca during the believer's lifetime.[8]

Prayer for the Muslim must be observed five times a day: daybreak, noon, mid-afternoon, sunset, and night. Prayer must not be entered into without first cleansing the body of any pollutants by washing with water the hands,

---

[8] Emory C. Bogle, *Islam – Origin & Belief* (Austin, TX: University of Texas Press – Austin, 1998), 26-36.

feet, head, neck, arms up to the elbows, and legs up to the knees. If water would not be available, then the believer could use unpolluted sand. After the worshipper is cleansed, he or she must fulfill specific requirements whenever he or she prays. He or she must align themselves to face Mecca and use a carpet, a piece of fabric, or even some leaves to provide a special surface upon which to pray. Virtually all individual or collective prayer includes a recitation of the first chapter *(surah)* of the Koran.

When a Muslim prays, he first starts in a standing position, then drops to a kneeling position and proceeds from there to as many as four prostrations. Each sequence of prostrations results in the worshipper on hands and knees with forehead and nose against the ground or floor. Each Muslim is required to attend Friday noon-day prayers as well.

As mentioned before, one of the Five Pillars of Islam is the requirement to make a pilgrimage to Mecca at least once in the believer's life time. The believer only has six days within each year to make the pilgrimage *(hajj),* and if the person performing the hajj has a proper penitent attitude, he or she will be free from sin following the pilgrimage.

During the hajj, the adherent will go to the Grand Mosque in Mecca for prayers and then circumambulate the Kaaba seven times in a counterclockwise direction. This circumambulating the Kaaba is to represent what Abraham was supposed to have done. (Judaism and Christianity do not teach this.) Then that day of the hajj the pilgrims proceed to Mina, a small city south of Mecca, and spend the night in prayer and meditation. The following day each pilgrim collects stones to throw at three pillars that represent the Devil and his two helpers who were supposed to have tempted Abraham to disobey God's command to sacrifice Ishmael.

After the time in the desert at Mina, the pilgrims have a large feast and then proceed to Mecca to circumambulate the Kaaba again seven times. Each pilgrim tries to touch or to kiss the Black Stone embedded in the corner of the Kaaba:

The Black Stone, or the Kaaba stone, is set on the outside of one corner of the Kaaba and is kissed by all pilgrims who can gain access to it. It is a dark, red brown, and now encased in a massive silver band. It is presumed to be of pre-Islamic origin, possibly meteoric. Myths claim that it fell from heaven, or perhaps that it was brought to earth by angels as a white stone in order to provide the cornerstone of the original Kaaba. It turned black by the impure touch of humans across the millennium. It is lovingly referred to as "the cornerstone of the House," or even the "right hand of God on earth." This stone was presented by Gabriel for the Kaaba and the people who worshipped within it. Muslims, in general, try to kiss, touch, or point to the Kaaba Stone, and often make circumambulations (tawaf) around it. Such circumambulations form, during the pilgrimage season, an integral part of the pilgrimage performance. This circumambulation is performed in the vicinity of the Kaaba, on the polished granite called the mataf. There is a place between the Black Stone and a raised door, against which pilgrims press their bodies in order to receive the blessings and powers that are associated with the holy house. Muslim peoples claim that it is not an idol to be worshipped, instead it is a special place from which to send prayers. The correct name for the Kaaba Stone is the Al-Hajarul Aswad.[9]

Another of the Five Pillars of faith is the requirement to profess their faith. This profession of their faith is found in the statement each believer proclaims: *"There is no god but Allah and Muhammad is his*

---

[9] http://www.salagram.net/kaba-stone.html

Prophet." This profession in Islam constitutes the one incontrovertible duty of all Muslims. Conversely, the unwillingness to acknowledge this belief constitutes *shirking* and the unforgivable transgression of Allah's law. Acceptance of Muhammad as Allah's prophet (or representative) is also essential to be a true believer in Islam.

Islam teaches that true worship of Allah must be in one's giving of money and wealth, a required 2.5% of a believer's net worth annually. This stands in contrast to Christianity, which teaches that believers should give at least 10% of their annual net worth. It is not required to be a follower of Jesus or to enter heaven, however.

As we have seen, Christianity and Islam stand on opposite ends in their beliefs and worship of God. Christianity teaches that it is what's in the heart, and rituals, special prayers and the works of religious practices do not please God. Yes, Christianity and denominations within Christianity do perform rituals and special prayers, but they are not an end within themselves.

Islam, on the contrary, teaches that it is rituals, prayers, and the workings of flesh that please their god Allah. If believers in Allah do not perform in a way that is pleasing to Allah or the Koran's teachings, they believe they will never enter paradise.

CHAPTER 8

DOES GOD REQUIRE BLOOD?

This chapter and its title draw attention to one of the great mysteries in most religions. The mystery that God would require blood shedding on behalf of those who would believe in Him and walk in His ways has plagued mankind ever since man has been worshipping any deity. In this chapter I will present Hebraic, Christian and Koranic/Muslim thought about the necessity for the shedding of blood.

Hebraic

The first blood shedding to appease God came soon after the creation of the earth. Jewish and Christian Scripture mention the fall of man and the sad necessity for the shedding of blood. The Koran does mention the sin and fall of man but does not mention the shedding of blood in association with Adam and Eve and goes as far as stating that God forgave Adam and Eve.

The book of Genesis gives a full account of the first shedding of blood. This sad occurrence happened after

Adam and Eve sinned by disobeying God and eating of the tree of knowledge of good and evil.[1] This act of their free will demonstrated that mankind would be willing to disregard God's commands, wisdom, and what is in mankind's best interests. Adam and Eve's nakedness represented purity and sinlessness before their sinful act. That sinlessness was a gift of God when He made all of creation and *"...saw that it was good."* Man, however, was given free will and choice, choice to choose God's way or to choose their own way upon the earth. Their choice would, however, propel them into greatness as God's crowning creation, walking with Him in obedience or bringing degradation because of their association with Satan and his degenerate lifestyle without God.

After Adam and Eve realized their changed state, without the covering of purity, they ran from the presence of God and hid in the garden. They tried to cover themselves with fig leaves, thereby doing for themselves only that which God could do, making themselves pure again as they were before their rebellion. God called out to Adam and Eve and made them come to grips with their disobedience and changed condition. God then killed an animal (this student believes it was a lamb) and covered our

---

[1] Gen. 3:21-22.

first parents with the skins from the sacrificed animal.[2] This was the first shedding of blood ever to have taken place to atone for sin. The animal's (lamb) innocence was sacrificed to cover sin. This event initiated the sacrificial system for setting aside man's sin.

The Old Covenant (Testament) includes a blood covenant with the Jews where their sins were covered over by the blood of innocent sacrifices of many thousands of animals:

The Noahadic covenant.

> *Then Noah built an altar to the Lord and, taking some of all the clean animals and clean birds, he sacrificed burnt offerings on it. The Lord smelled the pleasing aroma and said in his heart: "Never again will I curse the ground because of man, even though every inclination of his heart is evil from childhood. And never again will I destroy all living creatures, as I have done."*
> Gen 8:20-21

The Mosaic covenant.

> *The animals you choose must be year-old males without defect, and you may take them from the sheep or the goats. Take care of them until the fourteenth day of the month, when all the people of the community of*

---

[2] Gen. 3:21.

Israel must slaughter them at twilight. Then they are to take some of the blood and put it on the sides and tops of the doorframes of the houses where they eat the lambs. That same night they are to eat the meat roasted over the fire, along with bitter herbs, and bread made without yeast. Do not eat the meat raw or cooked in water, but roast it over the fire — head, legs and inner parts. Do not leave any of it till morning; if some is left till morning, you must burn it. This is how you are to eat it: with your cloak tucked into your belt, your sandals on your feet and your staff in your hand. Eat it in haste; it is the Lord's Passover. On that same night I will pass through Egypt and strike down every firstborn — both men and animals — and I will bring judgment on all the gods of Egypt. I am the Lord. The blood will be a sign for you on the houses where you are; and when I see the blood, I will pass over you. No destructive plague will touch you when I strike Egypt.

Ex 12:5-13

The Hebraic covenant.

Moses then took the blood, sprinkled it on the people and said, "This is the blood of the covenant that the Lord has made with you in accordance with all these words."

Ex 24:8

The Abrahamic covenant.

For the life of a creature is in the blood, and I have given it to you to make atonement for yourselves on the altar; it is the blood that makes atonement for one's life.

Lev 17:11-12

So the Lord said to him, "Bring me a heifer, a goat and a ram, each three years old, along with a dove and a young pigeon." Abram brought all these to him, cut them in two and arranged the halves opposite each other; the birds, however, he did not cut in half.

Gen 15:9-11

When the sun had set and darkness had fallen, a smoking firepot with a blazing torch appeared and passed between the pieces. On that day the Lord made a covenant with Abram and said, "To your descendants I give this land, from the river of Egypt to the great river, the Euphrates — the land of the Kenites, Kenizzites, Kadmonites, Hittites, Perizzites, Rephaites, Amorites, Canaanites, Girgashites and Jebusites."

The Lord made a covenant with Abram...

Gen 15:17-21

The Abrahamic Covenant is an unconditional covenant. God made promises to Abraham that required

105

nothing of Abraham. Genesis 15:18-21 describes a part of the Abrahamic Covenant, specifically dealing with the dimensions of the land God promised to Abraham and his descendants.

The actual Abrahamic Covenant is found in Genesis 12:1-3. The ceremony recorded in Genesis 15 indicates the unconditional nature of the covenant. The only time that both parties of a covenant would pass between the pieces of animals was when the fulfillment of the covenant was dependent upon both parties keeping commitments. Concerning the significance of God alone moving between the halves of the animals, it is to be noted that it is a smoking furnace and a flaming torch, representing God, not Abraham, who passed between the pieces. Such an act, it would seem, should be shared by both parties, but in this case it is doubtless to be explained by the fact that the covenant is principally a promise by God. He is the one who binds Himself. God caused a sleep to fall upon Abraham so that he would not be able to pass between the two halves of the animals. Fulfillment of the covenant fell to God alone.

The Solomon covenant.

> *The Lord was pleased that Solomon had asked for this. So God said to him, "Since*

you have asked for this and not for long life or wealth for yourself, nor have asked for the death of your enemies but for discernment in administering justice, I will do what you have asked. I will give you a wise and discerning heart, so that there will never have been anyone like you, nor will there ever be. Moreover, I will give you what you have not asked for — both riches and honor — so that in your lifetime you will have no equal among kings. And if you walk in my ways and obey my statutes and commands as David your father did, I will give you a long life." Then Solomon awoke — and he realized it had been a dream. He returned to Jerusalem, stood before the ark of the Lord's covenant and sacrificed burnt offerings and fellowship offerings. Then he gave a feast for all his court.

1 Kings 3:10-15

The Davidic covenant.

Ought ye not to know that the Lord God of Israel gave the kingdom over Israel to David for ever, even to him and to his sons...?

2 Chron 13:5

The Davidic Covenant refers to God's promises to David through Nathan the prophet and is found in 2 Samuel 7 and later summarized in 1 Chronicles 17:11-14 and 2 Chronicles 6:16. This is an unconditional covenant made between God and David through which God promises

David and Israel that the Messiah would come from the lineage of David and the tribe of Judah, and would establish a kingdom that would endure forever (2 Samuel 7:10-13). The Davidic Covenant is unconditional because God does not place any conditions of obedience upon its fulfillment. The surety of the promises made rests solely on God's faithfulness and does not depend at all on David's or Israel's obedience.

The Davidic Covenant centers on several key promises that are made to David. 1) God reaffirms the promise of the land that He made in the first two covenants with Israel (the Abrahamic and Mosaic Covenants). This promise is seen in 2 Samuel 7:10: *"Moreover I will appoint a place for My people Israel, and will plant them, that they may dwell in a place of their own and move no more; nor shall the sons of wickedness oppress them anymore, as previously."* 2) God promises that David's descendant or *"seed"* will succeed him as king of Israel and that David's throne will be established forever. This promise is seen in 2 Samuel 7:12-13: *"I will set up your seed after you, who will come from your body, and I will establish his kingdom. He shall build a house for My name, and I will establish the throne of his kingdom forever."* This is a reference to the coming Messiah.

The provisions of the covenant are summarized in 2 Samuel 7:16: *"And your house and your kingdom shall be established forever before you. Your throne shall be established forever."* The promise that David's *"house,"* *"kingdom"* and *"throne"* will be established forever is significant because it shows that the Messiah will come from the lineage of David and that He will establish a kingdom from which He will reign. The covenant is summarized by the words *"house,"* promising a dynasty in the lineage of David; *"kingdom,"* referring to a people who are governed by a king; *"throne,"* emphasizing the authority of the king's rule; and *"forever,"* emphasizing the eternal and unconditional nature of this promise to David and Israel.

Each of the covenants made by God to Adam's descendants was confirmed by blood through the sacrifice of an innocent animal. In each case those making the covenant with God understood that blood shedding was required because God required it.

The Old Covenant (Testament) is very clear that without the shedding of blood there is no sacrifice for sin.

For the life of a creature is in the blood, and I have given it to you to make atonement for yourselves on the altar; it is the blood that makes atonement for one's life.

Lev 17:11-

Moses then took the blood, sprinkled it on the people and said, "This is the blood of the covenant that the Lord has made with you in accordance with all these words."

Ex 24:8

Christian

As we study the New Covenant (Testament), we find Jesus coming as the Messiah[3] of God who will redeem mankind and cleanse the world of sin through a blood sacrifice of His own flesh. His shed blood fulfills the requirement of the Old Covenant and insures that mankind is brought back into son-ship as Adam was before his rebellion. The New Testament speaks very clearly of the blood sacrifice of Jesus and declares that He is the one of whom God spoke as Adam's and David's son.

For this is My blood of the new covenant, which is shed for many for the remission of sins.

Matthew 26:28

...we have redemption through His blood, the forgiveness of sins...

Ephesians 1:7

...having now been justified by His blood...

---

[3] מָשִׁיחַ (māšîaḥ)- anointed; - usually a consecrated person (as a king, priest); - specifically, the Messiah.

Romans 5:9

...without the shedding of blood there is no remission of sin.

Hebrews 9:22

...redeemed...with the precious blood of Christ...

1 Peter 1:19

Jesus claimed to be the one for whom the promises and covenants were made and through His sacrifice fulfilled the covenant on behalf of mankind. He spoke clearly of His mission to be the One who would take away the sins of mankind, and that His sacrifice would set all of humanity free from the affects of sin.

Think not that I am come to destroy the law, or the prophets: I am not come to destroy, but to fulfill.

Matthew 5:17

You diligently study the Scriptures because you think that by them you possess eternal life. These are the Scriptures that testify about me.

John 5:39

Koranic

The Koran claims to be the continuation of God's previous Scriptures and to be the final revelation to mankind. It claims that the Allah is the same God whom the Jews believe in and the Christians are supposed to believe in. The Koran even portrays Jews as special people through whom Allah sent prophets into the world.[4] These claims are continually reinforced in Surah 29:46, which reads, *"Our God and your God is one, and to Him we submit."* If this is true, then why do Muslims deny many of the Hebrew and Christian Scriptures and accept the belief that this same God would change what He first proclaimed about the requirement of blood to forgive sins?

Islam denies the sacrifice of Jesus and does not accept the fact of His death, resurrection and atonement for mankind's sin. The Koran completely denies that Jesus shed His blood to make atonement for mankind. The Koran teaches that the only thing that should matter to a Muslim is submission to Allah, and if Allah has mercy on him and he does many good works, he will find favor with Allah; the blood atonement made by anyone is not important. The only blood sacrifice that would be accepted is the sacrifice of a martyr while in jihad.

Jihad is interpreted by most devout Muslims as a physical fighting in the cause of Allah. Although many Muslims do not take part in jihad in battles for Allah, it is a requirement of Allah that Mohammad taught.

---

[4] Surah 2:47, 5:20.

112

Allah's apostle was asked, "what is the best deed?" The prophet replied "To believe in Allah and his Apostle." Then he added that the next best was to "participate in Jihad in Allah's cause."

Hadith 1:25

Apparently, the only requirement for Muslims to enter into paradise is their strict submissive obedience to Allah. Blood is not required for the forgiveness of sin, and good works would please Allah, and if enough of them were done, then maybe, just maybe, the submissive one would be accepted. However, if they would fight and die in Jihad, then the shedding of their blood would give them an entrance into paradise and the promise of wine, women and feast.

The Jihad, then, is one thing a Muslim would understand as a blood covenant with Allah.

Think not of those who are slain in Allah's way as dead. Nay, they live, finding their sustenance from their Lord. They rejoice in the Bounty provided by Allah...the (Martyrs) glory in the fact that on them is no fear, nor have they (cause to) grieve. They rejoice in the Grace and the Bounty from Allah, and in the fact that Allah suffereth not the reward of the Faithful to be lost (in the least).

Surah 3:169-71

113

Such passages as these provide much of the rationale for a further theological position: not only does a martyr in the cause of Allah enter paradise, but he does so automatically–his admission is guaranteed. Many hadith elaborate on this theme, such as this from *Sahih Bukhari*:

> *Allah's Apostle said, "Someone came to me from my Lord and gave me the news that if any of my followers dies worshipping none along with Allah, he will enter Paradise." I asked, "Even if he committed adultery and theft?" He replied, "Even if he committed adultery and theft."*
>
> Volume 2, Book 23, Number 329

Further rewards, as reported by hadith, are that the fighter in Allah's cause will, if killed in the struggle, receive privileges otherwise unattainable: he escapes the examination in the grave by the "interrogating angels"; he does not need to pass through *barzakh,* the purgatory limbo; he receives the highest of ranks in paradise, sitting near the throne of Allah. Muhammad described the "house of martyrs," *dar al-shuhada',* as the most beautiful abode of paradise; on the Day of Judgment any wounds the martyr received in battle will shine and smell like musk; his death as a martyr frees him of all sin, such that he does not require the intercession of the Prophet; he is purified by his act, and so he alone is not washed before burial. The popular understanding of the Quranic descriptions of this paradise for the believer (martyr or not) could not but be of the greatest appeal to the desert-dwelling nomad; awaiting him is a garden of cool breezes, beautiful companions, couches, fruit and drink, and nearness to Allah. Particularly deserving martyrs are even eligible for double the standard reward, some hadiths report. This is an incentive so great that Mohammad is reported to have said that no one who dies and enters paradise "would wish to come back to this world," even if he were to be given ownership of "the whole world and whatever is in it," except the martyr who, "on seeing the superiority of martyrdom, would like to come back to the world and get killed again." Finally, the martyr enacts the greatest act of worship possible for a human, for only he, the *shahid,* witnesses to, *shahida,* Allah Himself.

Islam does have other blood sacrifices, but they seem to be more for ritualistic reasons than for forgiveness of one's sins. There are two main occasions when Muslims enjoin a blood-sacrifice, namely, at the birth of a child and at the annual feast in Mecca, which is also celebrated in every Muslim community. The sacrifice for the birth of a child is like an initiation and the second is commemorative. When a child is born, the mullah or imam (priest) would say, *"O Allah, here is the aqiqa (sacrifice) for this son, its blood for his blood, its flesh for his flesh, its hair for his hair and save this son from the fire, etc."*

Edward Westmarck, in his two volume set, *The Origin and Development of the Moral Ideas,* tells of blood-sacrifices made by Muslims at the tombs of saints to secure their intercession; on the sea for a safe voyage; at the eclipse of the sun and moon; on the threshing-floor to bless the harvest; on taking a solemn oath, or even to consecrate a new market place in the village. [5] All these, however, seem to be like a talisman and are contrary to Biblical Scripture and against everything Jesus taught about the one sacrifice for sin: His own shed blood.

---

[5] Edward Westmarck, *The Origin and Development of the Moral Ideas* (London: MacMillan and Company, 1917), 387.

CHAPTER 9

THE NEW CHOSEN PEOPLE

As we study the Hebrew and Christian Scripture, we find that God chose a specific people through whom He would bring about His redemptive plan. These people, the Hebrews, were the people God chose to hear and record His word. (*PLEASE NOTE: Many are under the false impression that "the Jews" are God's Chosen, but this is not entirely true. "The Jews" has simply become a blanket description for all Israelites – but in actuality, only someone born into the Tribe of Judah can claim they are Jews. Remember, there were 12 Tribes, Yehudah {Judah/"the Jews"} being only one of them, albeit the "favored" one because Yehudah was charged with bringing Torah to the world. And don't forget, Jesus came from the Tribe of Yehudah. But the fact is, there were no Jews until after Jacob begat the Tribe of Yehudah {Genesis 29:35; Matthew 1:1-2}. The Tanach {OT} shows that His Chosen were called Hebrews {Genesis 12}, which means "to cross over.")* Through the Jews, God spoke to His prophets who in turn spoke to the people about the one true God and what His requirements were for purity, holiness and love.

Although the Jews were God's chosen people, they rebelled against His direct commands to be pure and separated people from the norm of societies of the earth. They turned from God and followed their own imaginations about the true living God. God, however, did not destroy or disregard His covenants that He made with the Jewish forefathers. He continued to direct the Jews to a place of prominence within His plan for mankind. They would be the ones from whom the whole world would be blessed.

> *Remember these things, O Jacob, for you are my servant, O Israel. I have made you, you are my servant; O Israel, I will not forget you.*
>
> Isa 44:21

> *May your eyes be open to your servant's plea and to the plea of your people Israel, and may you listen to them whenever they cry out to you. For you singled them out from all the nations of the world to be your own inheritance, just as you declared through your servant Moses when you, O Sovereign Lord, brought our fathers out of Egypt.*
>
> 1 Kings 8:52-53

But Zion said, "The Lord has forsaken me, the Lord has forgotten me." "Can a mother forget the baby at her breast and have no compassion on the child she has borne? Though she may forget, I will not forget you! See, I have engraved you on the palms of my hands; your walls are ever before me. Your sons hasten back, and those who laid you waste depart from you."

Isa 49:14-17

"I scattered them with a whirlwind among all the nations, where they were strangers. The land was left so desolate behind them that no one could come or go. This is how they made the pleasant land desolate." Again the word of the Lord Almighty came to me. This is what the Lord Almighty says: "I am very jealous for Zion; I am burning with jealousy for her." This is what the Lord says: "I will return to Zion and dwell in Jerusalem. Then Jerusalem will be called the City of Truth, and the mountain of the Lord Almighty will be called the Holy Mountain." This is what the Lord Almighty says: "Once again men and women of ripe old age will sit in the streets of Jerusalem, each with cane in hand because of his age. The city streets will be filled with boys and girls playing there." This is what the Lord Almighty says: "It may seem marvelous to the remnant of this people at that time, but will it seem marvelous to me?" declares the Lord Almighty. This is what the Lord Almighty says: "I will save my people from the countries of the east and the west. I will

bring them back to live in Jerusalem; they
will be my people, and I will be faithful and
righteous to them as their God."   Zech
7:14-8:8

The New Testament reaffirms the reality of the Old
Testament's declaration of the Jew as being God's chosen
people. Because God's word had been preserved for all
generations, the testament of God's promises to one nation
stands true even in the face of those who try to deny its
authenticity. The very word of God that the Jew preserved
is an indictment against anyone who would refuse its power
of credibility that had been passed down through time by
the Jew.

> *I speak the truth in Christ — I am not lying,*
> *my conscience confirms it in the Holy*
> *Spirit— I have great sorrow and unceasing*
> *anguish in my heart. For I could wish that I*
> *myself were cursed and cut off from Christ*
> *for the sake of my brothers, those of my own*
> *race, the people of Israel. Theirs is the*
> *adoption as sons; theirs the divine glory, the*
> *covenants, the receiving of the law, the*
> *temple worship and the promises. Theirs are*
> *the patriarchs, and from them is traced the*
> *human ancestry of Christ, who is God over*
> *all, forever praised! Amen.*
>   Rom 9:1-5

New Testament writers, under the unction of the
Spirit of God, cement the reality of the Jews' very

existence by their presence in the earth in these later times. History, both Biblical and historical, record the trek of the Jews throughout time:

- *The Jew would be exiled (70 -135 AD). (Deuteronomy 28:64)*
- *Israel would become a wasteland (135 – 1900s).*
- *The Jews would be scattered worldwide (135 – 1900s).*
- *The Jews would be persecuted worldwide (135 – 1900s).*
- *The Jews would have a worldwide impact (135 – 1900s).*
- *The Jews' identity as a group would be preserved (135 – 1900s).*
- *The Jews would return to their homeland (1900s).*
- *The Jews would have Israel again as their own country (1948 to present).*

The Scriptures declare the specialness of the Jewish people to God's plan; they truly are God's chosen people and stand in a special covenant.

The Koran and Muslims deny that the Jews are a chosen people. They refuse to accept the fact that Abraham's attempted sacrifice of Isaac was part of God's plan for the whole earth. To them, if Isaac was the promised son, then they would have no claim to their continued belief that the promises made to Abraham are valid for them. You see, as the Hebrew and Christian Scripture proclaim, Isaac was the favored son, and through Isaac came the Hebrew ancestry. If that were true, they would be denying the God of Abraham and His promised covenant made to and through Isaac, instead of Ishmael.

The Koran, in Surah 3:110, declares that the real chosen people in the earth are those who believe in Allah and his prophet Muhammad.

> *You (true believers in Islamic Monotheism, and real followers of Prophet Muhammad and his Sunnah) are the best of people ever raised up for mankind...had the people of the Scripture (Jews and Christians) believed, it would have been better for them.*

The Koran also teaches that the Jews were removed from their special place of honor to God and turned into pigs and monkeys.

> *So when they (the Jews) exceeded the limits of what they were prohibited, We (Allah) said to them: "Be you monkeys, despised and rejected."*
> Surah 7:166

> *Shall I inform you of something worse than that, regarding the recompense from Allah: those (Jews) who incurred the Curse of Allah and His Wrath, and those whom He transformed into monkeys and swines...*
> Surah 5:60

122

These wild accusations are never proven by the Koran, and the questions of when did Allah transform the Jews into monkeys and pigs, where did this happen, and was it the whole nation of the Jews or just a few, are never answered. Keep in mind, however, that the earlier revelations of Muhammad spoke of Allah protecting the Jews, not punishing them and making them his only chosen people.

> *O Children of Israel! Remember My Favor which I bestowed upon you and that I preferred you to the Alamin (mankind and jinn - devils).*
>
> Surah 2:27

Surah 2:27 is completely disregarded by later revelations of Muhammad when he found the Jews and Christian would not accept those revelations. Muhammad's protection of the Jews was withheld, and he even ordered the death of all Jews.

The sad irony with Islam being the religion of the true God and Muslims being His chosen people is that there is no ongoing revelation of that group of people or religion being used by Him to confirm its authenticity. With Judaism and Christianity, there is not only biblical evidence, but there is historical evidence, which supports its claim to be chosen of God to speak to mankind of His will and ways.

The evidence of God's choice of the Jew as His chosen people stands solid when the account of their prophetic pilgrimage throughout history is read. God chooses the Jew, uses the Jew, and confirms the Jew by fulfilling everything promised and solidifies it in the Jewish Messiah as He walked the earth.

CHAPTER 10

SALVATION

This chapter focuses on probably the greatest main theme of Christianity and Islam: whether the god of Muhammad, Allah, has a plan for mankind's salvation or whether the God of Abraham, Isaac, Jacob, Judah, Solomon, or David does. Either God has shown mankind and passed down through the centuries His revealed perfect plan or He hasn't. There must be one way, there must be no mistaking it, and it must be doable for mankind.

Christianity declares that God's plan was known before the foundations of the world. Islam declares that God's plans had to be changed because of mankind's wickedness. Muhammad states that God had to change His mind because men would not follow the first revelations passed down to them. Jesus states that God knew from the very beginning of creation what would be needed. These two religions face each other over the gulf of ignorance on one side and the clear light of proven revelation on other.

If Christianity has the answer for mankind's waywardness, it must present to the world a message that really changes the hearts of men. If Islam has the answer, then it must produce a message other than the sword. When all is said and done, one must answer the question, "How is a man saved and made right with God?" After all, eternity faces all humans, and what the end holds has intrigued mankind from its very beginning. If there is an eternal salvation for each person, it is most important that we know the path that must be taken.

Yes, the path we take does make a difference. If there is only one way, then it behooves us to know that way. Christianity's way is narrow but knowable; Islam's way demands more than any human can give. One is made simple in that it permits someone else to rectify, fulfill, and mend the gulf between a Holy God and an unholy sinner. The other hobbles its believers and makes works a sacrifice that could never be enough nor insulate the adherent from his or her inherent inner darkness.

Islam

Islam's teaching is elusive and leaves the believer always wondering if he has satisfied the demands of Allah. Allah comes across as arbitrary, and one never seems to understand what is required in finding peace, acceptance and eternal rest. This confusion comes from the Koran and the life of Muhammad. The many *hadits,* which are the sayings of Muhammad and his lifestyle, often contradict the Koran and never seem to put the average Muslim at rest.

Even Muhammad didn't seem to know his fate when his end would come. He was asked by his daughter, Fatima, what her and his fate would be. The so-called final prophet of mankind gave the following answer: "Say: I am no bringer of newfangled doctrine among the apostles, nor do I know what will be done with me or you..." (Surah 46:9 Abdullah Yusuf Ali translation). Can you imagine, this prophet who proclaimed to be the last great prophet from God was not sure of going to heaven himself?

Salvation and heaven does not seem to be a comforting reality by what the Koran teaches. It teaches that everyone, Muslim and non-Muslim, will go to hell. The Muslim may, in time, be released from hell if his deeds outweigh his sins, but even that is arbitrary and at the whim of Allah. There just doesn't seem to be any absolutes or promises.

> *But does not man call to mind that we created him before out of nothing? So by thy Lord, without doubt, we shall gather them together, and also the evil ones with them;*

then shall we bring them forth on their knees
round about hell;"
Not one of you but will pass over hell: this is
way of the Lord, a decree which must be
accomplished. But we shall save those who
guarded against evil, and we shall leave the
wrong doers therein, humbled to their knees.

Surah 19:67-68, 71-72

Allah even goes as far to say that everyone, Muslim
and jinn (devils), will end up in hell:

If we had so willed, we could certainly have
brought every souls its true guidance: but
the word from me will come true. I will fill
hell with jinns and men all together.

Surah 32:13

Those around Muhammad had the same misgivings
over their eternal home and questioned the honesty of Allah
in saving anyone. Sahih Bakhari, probably the most trusted
of Muhammad's men, feared his final destiny and said, *"If*
one of my feet were inside paradise, and the other one were
still out, I would not yet trust the cunning of Allah," and
"Every time I start to pray I imagine Allah standing in
front of me and the king of death behind me, the paradise to
my right and hell to my left side, and I do not know what

my God is going to do to me. [1] How sad for these men who claimed to serve a "most merciful god," yet feared he could not be trusted for their eternal rest.

In his hadith Sahih Bukhari, taught that a person's salvation or final destiny was up for grabs depending upon what an angel wrote before he was born.

> *Allah's Apostle, the true and truly inspired said, "(as regards your creation), every one of you is collected in the womb of his mother for the first forty days, and then he becomes a clot for a another forty days, and then a piece of flesh for another forty days. Then Allah sends an angel to write four words: He writes his deeds, time of his death, means of his livelihood, and whether he will be wretched or blessed (in religion). Then the soul is breathed into his body. So a man may do deeds characteristic of the people of the (Hell) Fire, so much so that there is only the distance of a cubit between him and it, and then what has been written (by the angel) surpasses, and so he starts doing deeds characteristic of the people of Paradise and enters Paradise. Similarly, a person may do deeds characteristic of the people of Paradise, so much so that there is only the distance of a cubit between him and it, and then what has been written (by the angel) surpasses, and he starts doing deeds of the*

---

[1] Dr. Haykyl, *Men Around the Messenger* (Cairo, Egypt: Dar Al-Nahadah Publishers, 1972).

people of the (Hell) Fire and enters the (Hell) Fire. "
Volume 4, Book 55, Number 549

Dr. Mark Gabriel summarizes Bukari's hadith like this: *Allah sends an angel to write down four facts about the person's life: (1) his deeds, (2) his time of death, (3) his means of livelihood, and (4) whether he will be wretched or blessed (meaning whether he will go to hell or paradise). "[2]*

How sad for an individual who really desires to live a holy and right life, not knowing whether his final end would be in hell just because an angel wrote that he would be a wretched soul and has hell for his home.

Salvation for those who question Allah's favor in this life and his arbitrary approach to that favor does seem to have a way around it, and this is martyrdom. It doesn't seem to matter what any angel wrote about one's life; if one chose to die for the case of Allah, then that person would be ushered into paradise and find many physical and sensual pleasures. These pleasures seem to be the main emphases, instead of finding oneself in the presence of Allah.

---

[2] Mark Gabriel, *Jesus and Muhammad – Profound Difference and Surprising Similarities* (Lake Mary, FL: Frontline – A Strang Company, 2004), 91-92.

They shall recline on jeweled couches face to face, and there shall wait on them immortal youths with bowls and ewers and a cup of purest wine, that will neither pain their heads nor take away their reason; with fruits of their own choice and flesh of fowls that they relish. And theirs shall be the dark eyed houris, chaste as hidden pearls: a guerdon for their deeds ...And we created the houris and made them virgins, loving companions for those on the right hand.

Surah 56:12-40

No wonder so many over the centuries have died in jihad believing that their salvation with its many sensual pleasures awaited them according to the Koran and their prophet Muhammad.

By the way, some Muslim commentators try to downplay the Koranic verses about the virgins mentioned in the Koran, stating that they are misinterpreted. Ibn Warrq, a pseudonym, in his book, *Virgins? What Virgins? And Other Essays,* declares that in every case those verses are correctly interpreted.[3]

Muslims, in general, believe that they must earn salvation. Emory C. Bogle teaches, *"In general, Muslims must earn salvation through living their faith in their daily*

---

[3] Ibn Warraq, *Virgins? What Virgins? And Other Essays* (Amherst, NY: Prometheus Books, 2010), 249.

131

lives, rather than through some cathartic process, spontaneous revelation, or intercession from earthly or heavenly helpers."[4] There it is again, man trying to earn salvation by being righteous and holy without the inner spiritual and soulish strength to do it.

Christianity

Christianity doesn't come out of nowhere in the historical trek of eternity; it is founded upon centuries of God-breathed revelation and fulfilled in His promised Son. Salvation's promised reality finds its first day of son-light when God informed Adam and Eve they would produce a child from whom all nations would be blessed.[5]

In direct contrast to Islam that teaches that man must earn salvation by works of righteousness, Christianity teaches that man can not earn a right relationship with God by works. It seems to be obvious to Christian thought that if man could be good enough to do the right works, he wouldn't need God's intervention to live forever and to be capable of holiness. Scripture teaches that a man's works, are like rags, without appeal and without strength.

---

[4] Emory C. Bogle, *Islam Origin & Belief* (Austin, TX: University of Texas Press, 1998), 26.

[5] See Chapter 2 *Beginnings.*

All of us have become like one who is unclean, and all our righteous acts are like filthy rags; we all shrivel up like a leaf, and like the wind our sins sweep us away.
Isa 64:6
David says the same thing when he speaks of the blessedness of the man to whom God credits righteousness apart from works:
Rom 4:6

For it is by grace you have been saved, through faith — and this not from yourselves, it is the gift of God—not by works, so that no one can boast.
Eph 2:8-9

Works, or doing right things, or completing some sort of religious practice, does not constitute salvation to Christians. Those *"works"* would, however, give a proof of the believer's state of faith towards the true living God. James the Apostle, under the unction of the Holy Spirit, penned the following words about faith and works:

What good is it, my brothers, if a man claims to have faith but has no deeds? Can such faith save him? Suppose a brother or sister is without clothes and daily food. If one of you says to him, "Go, I wish you well; keep warm and well fed," but does nothing about his physical needs, what good is it? In the same way, faith by itself, if it is not accompanied by action, is dead. But someone will say, "You have faith; I have deeds." Show me your faith without deeds,

133

and I will show you my faith by what I do.
You believe that there is one God. Good!
Even the demons believe that — and
shudder. You foolish man, do you want
evidence that faith without deeds is useless?
Was not our ancestor Abraham considered
righteous for what he did when he offered
his son Isaac on the altar? You see that his
faith and his actions were working together,
and his faith was made complete by what he
did. And the Scripture was fulfilled that
says, "Abraham believed God, and it was
credited to him as righteousness," and he
was called God's friend. You see that a
person is justified by what he does and not
by faith alone. In the same way, was not
even Rahab the prostitute considered
righteous for what she did when she gave
lodging to the spies and sent them off in a
different direction? As the body without the
spirit is dead, so faith without deeds is dead.
James 2:14-26

Since salvation is based on justification, it would be imperative for the believer to understand what is meant when one is *"justified by faith."* This truth eludes the average Muslim since the Koran does not teach justification. But in the Hebrew and Christian Scripture, justification is an understood state for the believer.

Justification's meaning:

In Hebrew the word is (ṣāḏaq) צָדַק-*which means to be (causatively, make) right (in a moral or forensic sense);*

In Greek the word is (dikaioō) δικαιόω - *to render (i.e. show or regard as) just or innocent.*

In other words, for the one who has been justified, he/she has a standing before God as one who has not sinned. Their sins and rebellion were not forgotten about or not taken into account; just the opposite would be true. Their sins and rebellion would be the reason for their justification. The sin would not be held against them because they now would be in a state of justification based upon what someone else did for them. God, in His mercy and love, understood that man could not redeem himself because he is tainted by sin and rebellion and, therefore, in need of being justified; like someone has said, *"Just as if they had not sinned."*

Jesus, to the Christian, is more than the Son of God; He is God's very sacrifice for mankind's sins. Since Scripture declares that sin requires a sacrifice without blemish and the taint of sin, someone who did not have sin must die to bring forgiveness and justification. All men are under the penalty of sin since all men are descendants of Adam.

> *But now he has appeared once for all at the end of the ages to do away with sin by the sacrifice of himself. Just as man is destined to die once, and after that to face judgment, so Christ was sacrificed once to take away the sins of many people; and he will appear a second time, not to bear sin, but to bring salvation to those who are waiting for him.*
> Heb 9:26-28
> *Therefore, when Christ came into the world, he said: "Sacrifice and offering you did not desire, but a body you prepared for me; with burnt offerings and sin offerings you were not pleased. Then I said, 'Here I am — it is written about me in the scroll — I have come to do your will, O God.'"*
>
> Heb 10:5-7

Jesus, God's Son, came to be the perfect sacrifice and to take man's sins and to bring mankind justification. But Jesus is more than God's Son, He also is the son of man. His birth, although miraculous through a virgin woman, also came by the same means as all humans do: through the human birth canal of a woman. This process makes Jesus human as well as heavenly. He then is mankind's brother, flesh of our flesh and bone of our bone. He was subject to the earthly environment and subject to the sin that is in the world. He had choice, likes and dislikes, joys and sorrows, but never was He any less God and was very much human. It was because He was human that He could be the sacrifice for mankind. Salvation could only come by the sacrifice of a human since a human, the father of the human race, Adam, sinned. It had to be the son of Adam who would redeem mankind.

> *Consequently, just as the result of one trespass was condemnation for all men, so also the result of one act of righteousness was justification that brings life for all men. For just as through the disobedience of the one man* (Adam) *the many were made sinners, so also through the obedience of the one man* (Jesus) *the many will be made righteous.*
>
> Rom 5:18-19

Salvation then comes by way of Jesus, mankind's perfect, one and only sacrifice. This salvation, not based upon works or religious practices, comes by way of faith and trust in God who covenanted with humanity through Adam, Abraham, Isaac, Israel and David. Jesus as a descendant of the patriarchs doesn't demand one's life or shedding of blood as He Himself shed the necessary blood for forgiveness and justification.

> *He did not enter by means of the blood of goats and calves; but he entered the Most Holy Place once for all by his own blood, having obtained eternal redemption. The*

137

blood of goats and bulls and the ashes of a heifer sprinkled on those who are ceremonially unclean sanctify them so that they are outwardly clean. How much more, then, will the blood of Christ, who through the eternal Spirit offered himself unblemished to God, cleanse our consciences from acts that lead to death, so that we may serve the living God! For this reason Christ is the mediator of a new covenant, that those who are called may receive the promised eternal inheritance — now that he has died as a ransom to set them free from the sins committed under the first covenant. Heb 9:12-15

Jesus came as God's perfect love gift, doing for mankind what they could not do for themselves. This very act stands in stark contrast with Islam that denies that God would have a son, much less send him to die for humanity. The sacrifice of Jesus screams out to the world and those who refuse to see the necessity of His deeds to come and believe. The saving reality of Jesus' life whispers through the Spirit, *"I love you!"*

Salvation then takes on a greater reality than just getting someone to heaven. Jesus' sacrifice, once received through the faith of a believer, does for them what no religion, especially Islam, could ever do.

Salvation's meaning:

In Hebrew: (yəšûʿāh) יְשׁוּעָה - *something saved, i.e. (abstractly) deliverance; - hence, aid, victory, prosperity;*

In Greek: (sōtēria) σωτηρία - *rescue or safety (physically or morally).*

Salvation in Christianity saves one from many things, besides just taking a person to heaven when they die, if they are believers in Jesus and His sacrifice on their behalf. Salvation saves the believer:

- From hell.
- From the wrath of God, which will be poured out upon the earth during the end times.
- From the eternal separation from God.
- From the corruption that is in the world, which promotes anti-God lifestyle.

The whole truth of what salvation does for the Christian believer brings into focus the totality of the great importance of what Jesus did. Salvation through God's Son, Jesus, then makes it possible to live a life that would be demanded by Allah. For without God's direct intervention, man could never live up to the strict standards that Muslims believe are required of them. Something else would be necessary to live a pious, holy, and righteous life. Salvation through Jesus is that something!

Salvation in Christianity not only brings forgiveness to the believer, it opens the door for God to literally live inside of the believer and help him to live the life that God desires. Through the salvation experience, the Christian believer becomes God's very temple.

> *For it is God who works in you to will and to act according to his good purpose.*
> Phil 2:13

> *Don't you know that you yourselves are God's temple and that God's Spirit lives in you?*
> 1 Cor 3:16

This very act of salvation brings the believer into a totally different position than the average Muslim could ever dream of believing. This act of salvation makes the Christian a child of God, which makes him/her a partner with God in His redemptive plan in the earth. We will discuss this in the next chapter on *Evangelism.*

CHAPTER 11

EVANGELISM

Evangelism for Islam and evangelism for Christianity come from two totally different understandings of God's heart and desire for mankind. Islam believes that submission to Allah is what is most important, and he isn't interested in relationship with any man. Christianity believes that evangelism's main aim is to bring people to God and to His perfect loving relationship.

When we try to understand the methods, the heart of the matter, and the requirements of evangelism, we must never lose sight of the person who is being approached. Evangelism can lose sight of people if it is done only to bring someone into the believer's group, church or religion. True evangelism must always consider the eternal plan of God and never be done for selfish reasons.

Islam

Islam's approach to evangelism comes from a dictatorial understanding instead of a loving understanding for the soul of the one approached. Islam has a history of doing evangelism by means of the sword. It mattered more to Muhammad that those who came to the knowledge of Allah came by way of pure submission without open knowledge or understanding of the why's and wherefore's.

Often when someone would ask a question why Muhammad did or said something he believed, the answer would be a pert, *"Because that is Allah's will!"* Questioning Islam and the will of Allah could get one killed if it meant that Allah would look bad.

The method for propagating Islam is cut and dry; it leaves no room for individuality, and it demands a strict adherence to the end result, making someone submit to Allah and Muhammad. The Koran teaches that Allah is the only god there is, Muhammad is his prophet, and evangelism must never deviate from those two dogmas.

Islam is a geopolitical as well as a theocratic religion, and evangelism comes from conquering people, cities, regions or countries and installing the rule of Allah. It gives no place or room for any thought that is outside of or contrary to the Koran and the will of Allah and Muhammad. When either an individual or a nation comes into contact with pure Islamic evangelism, there is only one of three choices that are acceptable. Those choices are accept Islam, pay the *jizya* (a poll-tax on non-Muslims) or war with Islam.

> *Fight those who believe not in Allah, and his apostle, nor acknowledge the religion of truth [even if they are] of the people of the book (this would mean Jews and Christians), until they pay jizya [humiliating tax] with willing submission, and feel themselves subdued.*
>
> Surah 9:29

The Muslim way of thinking, influenced by the Koran and the teachings of Muhammad, can not conceive of any other way than to force others to accept Islam. Any society, religion, or inquisitive thinking is a danger to Islam and can not be tolerated. Bruce Assaf in his book, *Behind The Veil of Radical Islam – The Coming War,* said:

> *America is perceived as a Christian nation or Christianity's child. Since Islam is perceived by Muslims as superior and more accurate, Christian influence and outreach through assistance to other nations is regarded as a danger and threat to the moral fabric of Islamic society.* [1]

Assaf rightly understands the mind set within Islam and its constant state of agitation caused by those who

---

[1] Bruce W. Assaf, *Behind The Veil of Radical Islam – The Coming War* (Belleville, Ontario, Canada, 2007), 20.

refuse to bow to its demands. Because the love equation is missing in Islam, the main mode of evangelism must be by force. All through Islam's history, the main evangelistic tool was force; the non-Muslim majorities throughout the Middle East, Africa and the other Eastern regions slowly succumbed to repression and harassment until the only way was to submit to Muhammad and his god. Robert Spencer says that it is a myth to think that Islam had no bellicose designs on their neighbors.[2]

Sayyid Qutb, the Egyptian Koranic commentator (1906-1966), said:

> *Islam, on the other hand, is people's worshipping Allah alone, and deriving concepts and beliefs, laws and regulations from the authority of Allah, and freeing themselves from the servitude to Allah's servants. This is the very nature of Islam and the nature of its role on earth.[3]*

> *Islam cannot accept any mixing with Jahiliyyah (the society of unbelievers). Either Islam will remain, or Jahiliyyah; no half-half situation is possible. Command belongs to Allah, or otherwise to Jahiliyyah; Allah's Shari'ah will prevail, or else people's*

[2] Robert Spencer, *The Politically Incorrect Guide to Islam (And The Crusades)* (Washington, DC: Regnery Publishing, Inc., 2002), 108.

[3] Sayyid Qutb, *The Right to Judge,* http://www.islamworld.net/docs/justice.html (accessed March 1, 2011).

*desires: "And if they do not respond to you,
then know that they only follow their own
lusts. And who is more astray than one who
follows his own lusts, without guidance from
Allah? Verily! Allah guides not the people
who are disobedient."*

Surah 28:50

*Do they then seek the judgment of (the Days
of) Ignorance? And who is better in
judgment than Allah for a people who have
firm faith.*

Surah5:50

*The foremost duty of Islam is to depose
Jahiliyyah from the leadership of man, with
the intention of raising human beings to that
high position which Allah has chosen for
him. This purpose is explained by Raba'i Bin
'Amer, when he replied to the Commander in
Chief of the Persian army, Rustum. Rustum
asked, "For what purpose have you come?"
Raba'i answered," Allah has sent us to bring
anyone who wishes from servitude to men
into the service of Allah alone, from the
narrowness of this world into the vastness of
this world and the Hereafter, from the
tyranny of religions into the justice of Islam.*

There can be no doubt about it, Islam's aim is to
subdue all peoples, nations and religions until each
succumb to Allah and Muhammad. Evangelism to Allah
apparently is wrapped up in a mind set that says,
"Everyone else is wrong and I have the right way. I will

force you to see my way." The sad reality is that Allah's way only seems to lead to dogged adherence to religious submission that doesn't have an end in sight. Then, when the individual's end does come, there is no promise of rest or release.

The spread of Islam continued by means of the sword up to and after Muhammad's death, even when there was no organized or sustained opposition, because that was the way of spreading the message of Islam (Submission).

To be fair, Islam teaches that spreading its faith by force is forbidden, this is true. However, the way Islam is propagated is by the force of its political and social hegemony[4] system. Conversion to Islam followed the imposition of that system as the *dhimmis*[5] began to feel their misery.

Even for those who are born to Muslims there doesn't seem to be a time when they could make their own decision to follow Islam or not. It is a custom in most Muslim families to pass on their religion to their children just by whispering in their child's ear and reciting a series

---

[4] Preponderant influence or authority over others: DOMINATION.

[5] (dhimmi (Arabic: ذمي [ˈðɪmːiː]), (collectively أهل الذمة *ahl al-dhimmah*, "the people of the *dhimma* or people of the contract")

of Arabic words. This could be just a custom, but the sad irony is that it comes to mean that the child accepted Islam and can never leave it.[6]

Evangelism has no room for second thoughts in Islam. Christianity is a heart religion, if one would want to call it a religion, and Islam is a head religion; one desires to speak to the heart through loving understanding and compassion, and the other demands that its adherents blindly stay put and not inquire about its validity.

> *Ask and it will be given to you; seek and you will find; knock and the door will be opened to you. For everyone who asks receives; he who seeks finds; and to him who knocks, the door will be opened.*
> Matt 7:7-8

> *Evil men do not understand justice, but those who seek the Lord understand it fully.*
> Prov 28:5

> *O ye who believe! Ask not questions about things which if made plain to you, may cause you trouble. Some people before you did ask such questions, and on that account lost their faith."*
> Surah 5:101-102.

---

[6] Susan Crimp and Joel Richardson, *Why We Left – Former Muslims Speak Out* (New York, NY: WND Books, Inc., 2008), 8.

The Holy Prophet himself forbade people to ask questions ...so do not try to probe into such things.

The Meaning of the Koran, Maududi,
vol. III, pgs. 76-77

The prophet was asked about things which he did not like, and when the questioner insisted, the Prophet got angry. (vol. 1, no. 92) The Prophet got angry and his cheeks or his face became red. (vol. 1, no. 91) Allah has hated you...[for] asking too many questions.

vol. 2, no. 555; and vol. 3, no. 591,
Bukhari's Hadith

No wonder we see violence being committed against anyone who either questions the foundation of Islam or the validity of Muhammad in modern times. Even making a joke or a characterization of Muhammad can bring a death sentence to the poor individual who would do such a thing. The reason why executing apostates has always been well-ensconced in Islamic law is that there is an indisputable record of Muhammad and his companions doing exactly that.

From the Hadith:

Bukhari (52:260) - *...The Prophet said, "If somebody (a Muslim) discards his religion, kill him."*

Bukhari (83:37) - *Allah's Apostle never killed anyone except in one of the following three situations: (1) A person who killed somebody unjustly, was killed (in Qisas,) (2) a married person who committed illegal sexual intercourse and (3) a man who fought against Allah and His Apostle and deserted Islam and became an apostate.*

Bukhari (84:57) - *[In the words of] Allah's Apostle, "Whoever changed his Islamic religion, then kill him."*

Bukhari (89:271) - *A man who embraces Islam, then reverts to Judaism is to be killed according to "the verdict of Allah and his apostle."*

Bukhari (84:58) - *There was a fettered man beside Abu Muisa. Mu'adh asked, "Who is this (man)?" "Abu Muisa said, "He was a Jew and became a Muslim and then reverted back to Judaism." Then Abu Muisa requested Mu'adh to sit down but Mu'adh said, "I will not sit down till he has been killed. This is the judgment of Allah and His Apostle (for such cases) and repeated it thrice.' Then Abu Musa ordered that the man be killed, and he was killed. Abu Musa added, "Then we discussed the night prayers."*

Bukhari (84:64-65) - *Allah's Apostle: "During the last days there will appear some young foolish people who will say the best words but their faith will not go beyond*

149

their throats (i.e. they will have no faith) and will go out from (leave) their religion as an arrow goes out of the game. So, wherever you find them, kill them, for whoever kills them shall have reward on the Day of Resurrection."

<u>Abu Dawud (4346)</u> - *Was not there a wise man among you who would stand up to him when he saw that I had withheld my hand from accepting his allegiance, and kill him? Muhammad is chastising his companions for allowing an apostate to "repent" under duress. (The person in question was Muhammad's former scribe who left him after doubting the authenticity of divine "revelations" upon finding out that he could suggest grammatical changes. He was brought back to Muhammad after having been captured in Medina).*

Reliance of the Traveller (Islamic Law) o8.1 - *When a person who has reached puberty and is sane voluntarily apostatizes from Islam, he deserves to be killed.*

Walid Shoebat, an ex-Muslim terrorist, in his book, *Why I Left Jihad – The Root of Terrorism and the Return of Radical Islam,* tells of his years as a Muslim terrorist.

I was born and raised in Beit Sahour, Bethlehem, in the West Bank. Hatred of Jews was my education, what I was taught each day by teachers and parents and the entire community. I knew nothing else, so I

*believed it was a righteous thing to grow up
and kill Jews.* [7]

One might say that Shoebat's story is an exception to the rule, and it is, in the sense that most Muslims would never leave Islam for fear of death, but Shoebat's upbringing is very common amongst Muslims. The methods used to convert, keep, and maintain Islam flow with hate and dogged submission to a system of lies and misinformation.

Christianity

Christianity, as I have stated, is a religion of the heart; it speaks to the searcher at a higher plane then just to his or her earthly and emotional needs. Evangelism in Christianity never denies the questions, doubts, and misgivings of those who are approached. It knows that the heart of the matter is its basic tenet of evangelism, which is the call of God to save one of His creations.

Jesus directed His disciples to go into the whole earth and teach mankind of the true loving God and Father of all humans. He declared a message of love and forgiveness and promoted a peace-loving reality that touched everything in the human experience. Jesus showed

---

[7] Walid Shoebat, *Why I Left Jihad – The Root of Terrorism and the Return of Radical Islam* (USA: Top Executive Media, 2005), 13.

the reality of God the Father and His concern for each individual. His message was one of understanding based upon His Son's life in the flesh. He proved He was a god of approachability and called everyone alike to partake of His glory.

Jesus' disciples were directed to teach mankind the same message He taught and lived. That message didn't deny the needs of the flesh, but it promoted the eternal as greater than the temporal. Jesus came to feed, set free, and mend, but His great aim was to change the heart of man. Evangelism, then, must do something other than just getting someone to paradise; it must bring paradise into the individual. By that change, each person could really understand and partake of God's holiness and perfection. It wasn't enough that people just submit to God's will, it was important that they truly understood and received the good that was in it for them. By that reality, each person would be a partaker of God's very nature.

Evangelism in Christianity is a clarion call to the heart of mankind to see the difference a relationship with God can make in the human experience. That experience then can become a way of life that touches everything and everyone who comes into its sphere of influence.

As you go, preach this message: "The kingdom of heaven is near." Heal the sick, raise the dead, cleanse those who have leprosy, drive out demons. Freely you have received, freely give.

Matt 10:7-9

And he said unto them, Go ye into all the world, and preach the gospel to every creature.

Mark 16:15 KJV

The Lord is not slow in keeping his promise, as some understand slowness. He is patient with you, not wanting anyone to perish, but everyone to come to repentance.

2 Peter 3:9

Christian evangelism demands that understanding, patience, and heartfelt concern for those being evangelized is never lost in the process.

He is able to deal gently with those who are ignorant and are going astray, since he himself is subject to weakness.

Heb 5:1-3

And the servant of the Lord must not strive; but be gentle unto all men, apt to teach, patient, In meekness instructing those that oppose themselves; if God peradventure will give them repentance to the acknowledging of the truth; And that they may recover themselves out of the snare of the devil, who are taken captive by him at his will.

Christian evangelism demands that we keep the real enemy in his place. The real enemy is the Devil. People, no matter who they are, where they come from, what color they are or which religion they are in must never be seen as our enemy. If we truly confess Jesus, then that confessing must mimic His love, life, and lessons of eternal acceptance towards all. Love, acceptance and forgiveness must be our living example and our evangelistic tool used to conquer ignorance and indifference.

Brother Andrew once told a Christian TV interviewer that we must not focus on people as our enemy.[8] He knew that if we focus on the wrong enemy, we then can justify our own personal prejudices, which could keep us from evangelizing them for the glory of God. Christianity's evangelism is an "All are welcome!" a "Whoever will" religion, and its focus is God's focus.

---

[8] Brother Andrew, *For The Love Of My Brothers* (Orange, CA: Bethany House Publishing, 1998), 208.

CHAPTER 12

CONCLUSION

Having researched the power of Christianity and the power of Islam to affect a human life and thereby affect the spiritual, social and moral makeup of any peoples requires that one come to a conclusion without prejudice. Everyone has prejudices in one form or another, including this student, but if one is honest, one must weigh all the facts and then come to a conclusion. Christianity has its faults; over the centuries there were people in all groups of Christianity who claimed to have the whole truth, but they failed in their daily and historical function of those assumed truths. Islam proclaims to be the one true religion and the last religion authorized by Allah. Islam claims there is only one true prophet of Islam and Allah, the prophet Muhammad. Each of these religions stands out in the historical record and has given a lasting legacy of those things each promotes.

Honesty requires that we give credit where credit is due, but the main avenue we must attach the most credit to, or lack thereof, is the spirituality of Christianity and Islam. Both Islam and Christianity have made an impact on the world in science and philosophy. It is important to keep in mind with these truths that it was individual people that made those impacts, and it may not have made any difference what their religion was. Also, most Islamic claims of their scientific and philosophical advancements over the centuries usually came by way of those who were either subjugated into Islam or Islam copied.[1] Christianity's main premise is that God is interested in humanity and did something to demonstrate that interest. Islam's main premise is that Allah is most interested in mankind submitting to him and accepting his prophet Muhammad. In each case, submission to God is required, but how that submission is taught, promoted and propagated makes an important difference.

Legacy Left and Ongoing

If we are to realize the efficacy of the Christian faith compared to Islam, we must know what that power is and the weakness of Islam. Legacy is a picture that can't be

---

[1] Robert Spencer, *The Politically Incorrect Guide to Islam (And the Crusades)* (Washington, DC: Regnery Publishing, 2005), 87-97.

hidden; it stands in a place for all to see. Legacy casts its shadow throughout history and helps form societies and transforms people into accomplices for good or bad. Christianity and Islam have a legacy that can not be denied nor covered up, as the results speak for themselves. What is that legacy? What has transpired through the centuries that gives evidence of one's power for good and one for bad? Who is it that demands our attention? And, should we truly consider one worthy of our interest, attention, and allegiance if it forcibly demands our loyalty?

Christianity woos humanity with the call of God's heart with, *"I have loved you with an everlasting love; I have drawn you with loving kindness."*[2] Islam and the Koran teach that there is no wooing of those who "must" come to Allah. The Koran shows that Allah does not love transgressors, does not love creatures that are ungrateful or wicked, does not love those who do wrong, and does not love the arrogant and the vainglorious.[3] This lack of love on Allah's part is littered throughout the Koran and has no admirable qualities associated with what one would believe God would desire from His creation. As a matter of fact, Allah demands that people love him first before he would

---

[2] Jeremiah 31:3.

[3] Surah 2:190, 2:276, 3:57, 140, 4:36.

love them, and love is never used as the primary motivation to draw someone close to him. It is the very real legacy of love in Christianity that separates it from Islam.

Another important legacy that Christianity and Islam have left upon the world is the legacy of blood. As mentioned in earlier chapters, Christianity is a very bloody religion, and blood is required and is the very essence of forgiveness. Islam, in one sense, is a bloodless religion, but in another sense, a very bloody religion. These two outstanding contrasts between Christianity and Islam differ in the use of blood and the application of that use.

Christianity teaches and understands that man's fall into sin separated mankind from God's relationship with Him and put a wedge that only a proper sacrifice could rectify. The Biblical mandate that it is blood that brings about the remission of sin requires someone, a human, who must shed blood to bring forgiveness.[4] The blood that is required must be perfect and not contaminated with sin itself. Therefore, God, in His mercy, love and understanding, provided a way for the perfect blood to be shed for the remission of sin. He provided through His Son, Jesus.

---

[4] Hebrews 9:22 *In fact, the law requires that nearly everything be cleansed with blood, and without the shedding of blood there is no forgiveness.*

Blood Equation

Islam teaches that blood is not required for forgiveness of sin, but a total sold out attitude of heart and mind is. Submission by the Muslim believer is the foundation of forgiveness in Islam. The submission that is required must come from the believer without Allah's help, and that submission must be in constant and repetitive actions. The completion of works of many kinds may lend Allah's ear toward the believer, but nothing is promised, and even hell awaits all those who even submit to the best of their own frail abilities. So, we see, blood is not required, but there is no other way of forgiveness or acceptability other than submission. However, Islam is a very bloody religion in that it has mostly propagated itself through the means of the sword. The only blood-letting that would seem to please Allah is the blood of a person who would die in fighting for Allah.

> *Think not of those who are slain in Allah's way as dead. Nay, they live, finding their sustenance from their Lord. They rejoice in the Bounty provided by Allah...the (Martyrs) glory in the fact that on them is no fear, nor have they (cause to) grieve. They rejoice in the Grace and the Bounty from Allah, and in the fact that Allah suffereth not the reward of the Faithful to be lost (in the least).*
> Surah 3:169-171.

159

So, we see that the legacy of blood brought by Islam upon the world has been throughout its history, and the legacy of the blood realized through Christianity came by way of one person, Jesus of Nazareth, God's Son. Even today, 2011, we see the blood-letting on behalf of Allah's adherents and forced upon those who would disagree with his message. Women are killed because they were raped[5] and didn't follow the Koranic law of having a male relative with them at all times, people are killed because they dare to speak against Allah and Muhammad, and nations are attacked because they refuse to permit Muslims special Sharia law.

Son Equation

Christianity requires a Son of God. Islam denies that a son is required and by that denial has no efficacy to bring life to the believer. Christianity teaches that each person can have the life God intended by means of His Son Jesus. *"For as the Father has life in himself, so he has granted the Son to have life in himself," (John 5:26-27)* and *"And this is the testimony: God has given us eternal life, and this life is in his Son. He who has the Son has life; he*

---

[5] Chris McGreat, "Rape victim, 13, stoned to death in Somalia," *Guardin.co.uk*, 2 November 2008, http://www.guardian.co.uk/world/2008/nov/02/somalia-gender (accessed March 15, 2011). See Appendix D.

who does not have the Son of God does not have life," (1 John 5:11-12). This truth is always realized when someone truly believes this truth and turns to God for the application of it. Testimony after testimony can be found throughout the Christian world as to the life-changing affects of believing in the Son of God. In contrast to the belief in a Son of God, for those who deny that God has a Son who was sacrificed for mankind's sin, there is no satisfying reality of forgiveness or acceptance by God. In fact, there are many books written and compiled by ex-Muslims about why they left Islam. The running theme in most of the accounts was their lack of comfort in Allah and never knowing of their forgiveness; but when introduced to Jesus, as God's Son, they believed the message of forgiveness and found peace.[6]

Whose Ability?

The efficacy of Christianity over Islam can be realized in the belief in whose ability it takes to be saved. In Islam it is taught that any forgiveness, correction, or change must dwell within the believer. Through the many repetitive actions on the part of the Muslim, he/she may

---

[6] Susan Crimp and Joel Richardson, *Why We Left – Former Muslims Speak Out,* (LA, CA: WND Books, 2008.; Shoebat, Walid, *Why I Left Jihad,* (USA: Top Executive Media), 2005.; Gabriel, Mark, *Jesus and Muhammad – Profound Differences and Surprising Similarities,* (Lake Mary, FL: Frontline Publishing, 2004).

find pleasure with Allah and find some sort of acceptance. The repetitive actions are the Five Pillars of faith; (1) Profess their faith *(shahadah)* at all times; (2) Perform five daily prayers *(salat)*; (3) Annually contribute alms *(zakat)*; (4) Annually perform a thirty-day fast *(siyam)*; and (5) Make at least one pilgrimage *(hajj)* to Mecca during the believer's lifetime. But it should never be forgotten that it all depends on one's own abilities to make this a reality. However, in Christianity, it all depends on God's ability, not man's, because man can not because he is weak through the flesh, emotions and soul. God's requirement for perfection is too great for man to fulfill.

Christianity teaches that God made a way through His Son to come to man and then into man in order to give him the ability to live the requirements of righteousness and holiness.

> *For what the law could not do, in that it was weak through the flesh, God sending his own Son in the likeness of sinful flesh, and for sin, condemned sin in the flesh: That the righteousness of the law might be fulfilled in us, who walk not after the flesh, but after the Spirit. For they that are after the flesh do mind the things of the flesh; but they that are after the Spirit the things of the Spirit. For to be carnally minded is death; but to be spiritually minded is life and peace. Because the carnal mind is enmity against God: for it*

*is not subject to the law of God, neither
indeed can be. So then they that are in the
flesh cannot please God. But ye are not in
the flesh, but in the Spirit, if so be that the
Spirit of God dwell in you. Now if any man
have not the Spirit of Christ, he is none of
his. And if Christ be in you, the body is dead
because of sin; but the Spirit is life because
of righteousness. But if the Spirit of him that
raised up Jesus from the dead dwell in you,
he that raised up Christ from the dead shall
also quicken your mortal bodies by his Spirit
that dwelleth in you.*

Romans 8:3-11 KJV

What Evidence in History and Geography?

History records the way of Christianity and the way of Islam and maps out the course each took in its quest to touch mankind for God's glory. Islam, which I have proven, made its way into history through the man Muhammad, who made himself a prophet of Allah. Christianity rests on the centuries of people, places, and events that fulfilled many ancient writings and promises found in the Hebraic/Christian Scripture. Islam took for itself a title that was contrary to the ancient writings which came before it. Islam titled itself as the "Only true religion" while Christianity takes no such title, but rather cries, *"Come, taste and see!"*

163

Islam to this very day stands in the face of opposition with its fist in the air and cries, *"I dare you to question, deny or refuse!"* Even amongst its own people, those of the same bent and leaning, Islam fights to be accepted and submitted to. In most of the Muslim nations, there are wars and rumors of wars. At the present time, March 2011, almost every Muslim nation in Northern Africa and the Middle East, and most Muslim nations surrounding Israel are in conflict in one way or the other. These conflicts are nothing new for Islam and its history, as its history is filled with centuries of conflict and subjugation.

Christianity, for the most part, has never thought of war as a means to propagate its tenets, although some individuals have in times past used their conquest to teach Christianity to the local population. War, as a whole, in Christianity is not a choice for evangelism or the winning of populations. Christianity has spread throughout the world by means of its nature of love. In each case, when Christianity touches an individual or nation, we see compassion, generosity, and freedom. These three attributes come from the belief in a God who cares and desires the best for each individual. Even in a war setting Christianity requires compassion and understanding;

You have heard that it was said, "Love your neighbor and hate your enemy." But I tell you: Love your enemies and pray for those who persecute you, that you may be sons of your Father in heaven. He causes his sun to rise on the evil and the good, and sends rain on the righteous and the unrighteous.

Matthew 5:43-46.

Generosity seems to flow very easily from Christians and Christian-thinking nations throughout time: *"Do not judge, and you will not be judged. Do not condemn, and you will not be condemned. Forgive, and you will be forgiven. Give, and it will be given to you. A good measure, pressed down, shaken together and running over, will be poured into your lap. For with the measure you use, it will be measured to you" (Luke 6:37-3)* and *"Give to the one who asks you, and do not turn away from the one who wants to borrow from you" (Matthew 5:42).* Freedom and its basic belief found in Scripture stands out as a hallmark when Christian-style democracy comes to nations that before hand did not understand its principles; *"It is for freedom that Christ has set us free. Stand firm, then, and do not let yourselves be burdened again by a yoke of slavery" (Galatians 5:1).* We must understand that the freedom that Galatians 5:1 is speaking of is first the freedom from sin, which destroys fellowship with God, but also speaks of freedom to worship

165

God and to be free from those who would lead one astray to foreign gods.

Even today the historical records record the cry from many throughout the Muslim nations for the overthrow of democratic nations and the submission to Sharia law. The adherence to the strict Islamic thinking, sadly, has become the voice heard above those who take a more moderate stance in Islam. "Jihad" has become the cry for those who think they are being mistreated, but with no real proof of that mistreatment. Most of those who cry for Jihad do not even understand what they are crying war for.

Freedom

Christianity, from its beginnings, has set millions of captives free. You might say that Christianity has been the great liberator of the world. During the 2nd and 3rd centuries, tens of thousands of slaves were freed by people who converted to Christ. Throughout the Middle Ages, Christians and church councils freed slaves and forbid the mentality of slavery as a whole. One can not say this about Islam throughout the centuries as Islam was the main cause and perpetrator of slavery. Islam's very beginning is riddled with slavery, which supplied female slaves to the many harems of rulers and rich individuals. Black and white slaves from many parts of the world were taken to be used as eunuchs[7] in the court and harems of rulers. Slaves in general were made to work in hard labor and usually had no rights, but were treated as chattel. The Koran makes numerous references to slaves and slavery (Surah 2.178; 16.75; 30.28).

Christianity has also sanctioned slavery, but as a whole those slaves would have never been supplied if it were not for Islamic believers throughout the Muslim nations. Even when England and Europe stopped the slave trade, Muslim nations still subjugated peoples to its demoralizing realities. American's slave trade is a sad blight upon its Christian heritage that forbade its practice. However, there were many Christians within the American society that fought hard to abolish slavery and finally won at the end of the Civil War.

The Major Differences

Obviously there is a great gulf between Christianity and Islam. Obviously, those differences mean spiritual life

---

[7] A **eunuch** (pronounced /'juːnək/; Greek: "Eυνούχος") is a castrated man, usually one castrated early enough to have major hormonal consequences. A eunuch would likely be a servant or a slave who, because of his function, had been castrated, usually in order to make him safer servants of a royal court where physical access to the ruler could wield great influence.

or death to the believer, and one would be wise knowing those differences. There can't be any acceptable compromises when one considers either Christianity or Islam; one must be accepted and one must be rejected. Either Allah is God or he is a liar, either Jesus is who He claimed to be and the Bible is the Word of God, or it isn't. I say it is!

The foundation of Christianity is Jesus, the Son of God, who is both God and man. He declared Himself to be both, and He declared that His declaration would be realized to those who received His message and forgiveness. Love was Jesus' declaration of the heart of the Father, and then He proved it in His life, works and actions. Islam totally denies that Jesus was God's Son and demands death to anyone who promotes that tenet. To Islam, there is no room for a savior, much less a Son of God, as Allah has given Muhammad as his representative on Earth. Muslims believe that there is no messenger, prophet, or proclaimer of truth other than Muhammad. Christianity totally denies Muhammad and the Koran and sees Islam and Allah as the spirit of anti-Christ.

Jesus stands at the crossroad of history, time and eternity. It is imperative that every human come to know this truth. The efficacy of Christianity is only found in

Jesus and His sacrificial death for mankind. No man in history, no religion founded by man, and no demonic usurper can overcome the power of who Jesus is.

Jesus and Muhammad

Jesus claimed to be from God, the Son of God and the Word sent from God to proclaim the freedom of God. If this is so, we must see His standards and His works in light of Muhammad and his life:[8]

Jesus	*Muhammad*
■ The Prince of Peace.	■ Prophet of war.
■ Disciples were killed for their faith.	■ Disciples killed for their faith.
■ Forgave and converted his persecutors.	■ Promoted persecution.
■ Giver of life.	■ Took many lives.
■ Murdered none but saved many.	■ Murdered thousands.
■ Conversion by love and acceptance.	■ Conversion by compulsion.
■ Preached faith and peace.	■ Practiced force.
■ A deliverer.	■ A warrior.

---

[8] Peter Hammond, *Slavery, Terrorism and Islam* (USA: Xulonpress, 2010), 201-202.

▪ Said, *"Believe and live!"*	▪ Said, *"Convert or die!"*
▪ Shed His own blood for all.	▪ Swift to shed blood.
▪ Prayer for forgiveness of everyone.	▪ Preach death to infidels.
▪ Achieved a holy victory on the cross.	▪ Declared holy war (Jihad) against infidels.
▪ Constrained people through love.	▪ Constrained people through conquest.
▪ Called His disciples to love and not fight.	▪ Called his disciples to fight and kill.
▪ Ordered His followers to love the Jews and to preach the gospel to them.	▪ Ordered his followers to kill Jews.
▪ Mission to conquer sin's penalty and power.	▪ Mission to conquer the world for Allah.
▪ Claimed to be God.	▪ Claimed that there is no God but Allah.
▪ His tomb is empty!	▪ His tomb is occupied!

A Trail of Destruction

170

Islam's past can not be denied; history is its indelible witness as are those who succumbed to its demonic demands. A trail of destruction, starting from Islam's beginnings to the present, draws our attention to the reality that Islam is demanding worship that it has no right to demand. That trail of destruction encompasses the invasion of Syria in 634 AD where thousands of Christians were massacred. Then it traveled to Egypt, Cyprus, more of North Africa and Tripoli, where Christian women and children were forced into slavery. India came under the sword in 712 AD, and millions of Indians were enslaved, killed or raped, and it didn't matter what religion the people were. Again, in 1193 AD, more Buddhists were put to the sword, and they lost famous libraries and precious places. History shows that Spain, under the Moors, killed thousands; all of the Jews of Grenada were slaughtered and Christians deported to Morocco. The Holy Land saw the destruction of the Holy Sepulcher, and many Christian places of worship in Jerusalem were destroyed. Constantinople was lost to the Muslim invasion in 1453 AD, and the population was slaughtered even in the Hagia Sophia, the greatest Christian church in the world at that time. The Islamic Turks massacred hundred of thousands of Christians in Lebanon, Bulgaria, Armenia, and even in

1922, the Turks destroyed the ancient city of Smyra with its 300,000 Christian population. In 2010 thousands of Sudanesse Christians have been killed by Muslim armies who find favor with the government.[9] Even as of March 14, 2011, there are Christians being killed by Muslim extremists in the nation of Ethiopia.

> ADDIS ABABA, ETHIOPIA (Worthy News)-- *Thousands of Christians are fleeing violence in western Ethiopia where Muslim extremists killed several Christians and burned dozens of churches, rights activists and officials said. Advocacy group Barnabas Fund, which supports Christians in the Muslim-majority area, told Worthy News that 55 churches and dozens of homes are reported to have been torched in recent days near the city of Jimma, in western Oromia region, with many more properties looted by the mob.*[10]

With all of the information at hand, found throughout history and modern times, there is one

---

[9] Stefan Bos, Sudan Christians Urge Prayers Amid Widespread Killings, Worthy News.com, 2011, http://www.worthynews.com/6616-sudan-christians-urge-prayers-amid-widespread-killings (accessed March 15, 2011).

[10] Stefan Bos, *Thousands of Christians Flee Deadly Violence in Ethopia; Chruches Burned,* Worthy News.com, 2011, http://www.worthynews.com/10058-thousands-of-christians-flee-deadly-violence-in-ethiopia-churches-burned (accessed March 15, 2011).

conclusion of the matter of the efficacy of the Christian faith as compared with Islam; Islam is weak and does not have any power to bring a person to the saving knowledge of God. Nor does Islam meet the requirements of the ancient writings as being a forerunner of truth. The god, Allah, is found wanting in that he does not love, he teaches hate, and he denies the testimony of God's one and only Son, Jesus.

We have seen that Christianity liberates those who come under its blanket of love. Christianity draws a person to God with a clarion call of God's love. Christianity brings freedom to all aspects of the believer's life and promotes peace, not by repetitive works but the wooing of God's Spirit.

Islam makes captives of those who find it or are coerced into its fold. It belittles women and demeans their worth. It promotes death, and it accepts lying, cheating, and intolerance. All in all, one can not really compare Christianity and Islam as they are in two different camps. One is in the camp of life and the other in the camp of death.

> *This day I call heaven and earth as witnesses against you that I have set before you life and death, blessings and curses. Now choose life, so that you and your*

children may live and that you may love the Lord your God, listen to his voice, and hold fast to him. For the Lord is your life, and he will give you many years in the land he swore to give to your fathers, Abraham, Isaac and Jacob

Deut 30:19-20

CHAPTER 13

THE ECCLESIA

This chapter came after I readied this book for its final proof before sending it to the publisher. In the course of waiting on other authors to write endorsements for this book, I was given two CD's by a pastor friend, Sherry Hill. Sherry told me that she had listened to the teachings of Dutch Sheets,[1] from a Pastors' Summit, 2-25-2011, and it had made an impact upon her ministry. I must say, making an impact, for me, was an understatement. Sheets' teaching on the true nature of the Church and its authority and power falls right in line with the conclusion of this book. I believe that I have proven that Christianity's efficacy far surpasses Islam and can be the only true faith a person must believe in.

---

[1] Dutch Sheets is an internationally known speaker and author. He has written many books including the best seller *Intercessory Prayer*. For 18 years, Dutch has pastured Freedom Congregation in Colorado Springs, CO.

Dutch Sheets' premise for his teaching on the Church is founded upon the meaning of the word **ecclesia** or **ekklesia,** which Jesus used in Matthew 16: 13-20.

*The **ecclesia** or **ekklesia** (<u>Greek</u>: ἐκκλησία) was the principal assembly of the <u>democracy</u> of ancient <u>Athens</u> during its "<u>Golden Age</u>" (<u>480–404</u> BC). It was the popular assembly, opened to all male citizens over the age of 18 by <u>Solon</u> in <u>594 BC</u> meaning that all classes of citizens in Athens were able to participate, even the <u>thetes</u>. The ekklesia opened the doors for all citizens, regardless of class, to nominate and vote for magistrates—indirectly voting for the <u>Areopagus</u>—have the final decision on legislation, war and peace, and have the right to call magistrates to account after their year of office. In the 5th century BC their numbers amounted to about 43,000 people. However, only those wealthy enough to spend much of their time away from home would have been able to participate until <u>Pericles</u>' reforms in early 451-2 BC allowing payment for jurors. The assembly was responsible for declaring war, military strategy, and electing <u>strategoi</u> and other officials. It originally met once every month, but later it met three or four times per month. The agenda for the ekklesia was established by the <u>Boule</u>, the popular council. Votes were taken by a show of hands.*[2]

---

[2] R. K. Sinclair, (1988). *Democracy and participation in Athens*. <u>Cambridge University Press</u>. <u>ISBN</u> <u>0521423899</u>

Thus, two of the most prestigious word resources in the English language confirm the fact that an "ecclesia" was originally a select civil body, summoned or convoked for a particular purpose. What, then, did the writers of the New Testament mean when they used the word "ecclesia" to describe a Christian body of people? We can assume that they intended to convey the original Greek meaning of the word: a body of Christians called out of the Roman and Judean system to come together into a separate civil community. It meant a politically autonomous body of Christians under no king but Jesus; under no other jurisdiction but that of Jesus. No man ruled them! Only Christ. And that was the reason these same Christians ran into trouble with kings and rulers; were arrested, crucified and martyred. They dropped Caesar as their King and took up Christ. When you consider the fact that an "ecclesia" was "a civil body politic", this is strong proof that the Christian ecclesias we read about in the New Testament were independent civil bodies of Christians - independent from worldly kings and governors, ruled by the Theocratic government of God's Spirit. They wanted freedom to serve King Jesus. They weren't building and attending churches! Please understand! The pattern laid down in the New Testament bears no resemblence to what we know today as "church". God's people are meant to live by the ecclesia

177

pattern -together in communities, holding all things in common, under the government of God through His anointed leaders. Quit saying "church" when it is supposed to be "ecclesia"! It's an important step in retrieving your brain from the trap of religious confusion. Independent self-government under Christ! That is what the ecclesia represents – not a religious organization for meeting on weekends.[3]

With the above information in mind, I would like the reader to see the importance, authority, and power the believers in Jesus have in the earth.

If every Christian believer would understand his or her place in the Kingdom of God and the great impact that each could make and then follow through with that understanding, there is no telling what changes the "Ecclesia" of God could make.

When a person turns to the Lord Jesus and then realizes his or her place in God's plan of redemption, using the authority and power available through his or her faith, things begin to change. Since each child of God has been given the mandate to *"go into the whole Earth and preach*

---

[3] John Thiel, *The word Ekklesia* http://sabbathsermons.com/2009/10/25/the-word-ekklesia/ (accessed 4/9/2011).

the gospel," it is important that each child knows his or her authority.

> *He said to them, "Go into all the world and preach the good news to all creation. Whoever believes and is baptized will be saved, but whoever does not believe will be condemned. And these signs will accompany those who believe: In my name they will drive out demons; they will speak in new tongues; they will pick up snakes with their hands; and when they drink deadly poison, it will not hurt them at all; they will place their hands on sick people, and they will get well."*
>
> Mark 16: 15-18

That authority gives the believer the power to not only preach the gospel of love and forgiveness, but it gives power over demons (the enemy), it releases spiritual gifts that make it possible to affect spiritual forces and realities, and it brings the healing ministry of Jesus into the realm of this world. All of this, of course, is only made real to the believer if he or she will truly "believe" and practice that authority.

In ancient times and, of course, in Jesus' age, everyone knew what the "ecclesia" was all about. It was a governmental authoritative body of people who made decisions that affected the whole of society. Jesus was telling the believers in Matthew 16: 13-16 that His "ecclesia" would have authority, under Him, to make changes and bring the Kingdom of Heaven to the realm of the earth.

When Jesus came into the coasts of Caesarea Philippi, he asked his disciples, saying, Whom do men say that I the Son of man am? And they said, Some say that thou art John the Baptist: some, Elias; and others, Jeremias, or one of the prophets. He saith unto them, But whom say ye that I am? And Simon Peter answered and said, Thou art the Christ, the Son of the living God. And Jesus answered and said unto him, Blessed art thou, Simon Barjona: for flesh and blood hath not revealed it unto thee, but my Father which is in heaven. (This was a Kingdom Communication.) *And I say also unto thee, That thou art Peter, and upon this* rock [the rock, is the method of Kingdom communication] *I will build my church [ecclesia]; and the gates of hell shall not prevail against it. And I will give unto thee the keys of The Kingdom of Heaven:* ("keys" grant access to the King-Dominion) *and whatsoever thou shalt bind on earth shall be bound in heaven: and whatsoever thou shalt loose on earth shall be loosed in heaven.* (This statement has been somewhat misunderstood in the religion of Christianity; it means that what you see in heaven is what shall be done on the earth [Matthew 6:10, Luke 11:2, John 5:36, John 9:4]. Peter saw that Jesus was the Christ in Heaven so to speak; he responded to The Kingdom of Heaven's communication

about who Jesus was. Jesus then affirms this
communication.)

Matthew 16:13-19 KJV

With this in mind, I want you to see the great importance
that you and every believer has to God's plan for the earth.
Christianity's power lies in its relationship to Jesus and the
authority He has given to each citizen within the "Ecclesia"
of the Kingdom. We are not a weak, defenseless group of
like minded-individuals; we are a glorious conglomerate
group of saved and empowered people to do exploits for
God.

Along with other powers, we have the power of
prayer, the words of our mouth that speak of our testimony
and declare with spiritual authority for demonic obstacles
to move aside, and the ability to loose and bind for God.

When a group of believers pray collectively the
prayers of authority, they will get results, for Scripture
declares it so:

> ...The effectual fervent prayer of a righteous
> man availeth much.

James 5:16 KJV

When a Christian-believing people know from
whence a spiritual obstacle comes, they can declare with
faithful confidence that the mountain of trouble or the

181

planted negative doubts be uprooted and gone, and it will be so!

When the God-centered congregation of like-minded siblings of Christ stand for righteousness and holiness and demand, through faith, that which is in heaven be established on Earth as it is in heaven, it will be so!

We must take our place, with the authority we have been given and make changes in our region of God's Kingdom upon Earth in which we have been planted. Islam is not, nor is any other religion, the one true authority in Earth, Christianity is! It is imperative that each Christian believer come to grips with that truth and live accordingly.

Our thinking within Christendom must change or we will fall prey to weak thinking and powerless activities that do nothing to promote righteousness and world changing reality. We, the "Ecclesia" of God, are the ones with the plan, the reality of God's life, and the over-riding collective vote to make a difference in all realms of society and spiritual reality. By vote, I mean that if we will get together as one whole and not separate identities, we will see changes in the areas (communities, counties, states, and country) in which we are planted.

We must be like the conquering Roman government that sent their "ecclesia" *(the governing body of officials who would rule and bring change to the newly-conquered nation or area)* to bring about change. The change we bring is the change founded upon the Scriptures, the Spirit, and the Life of God.

We must understand that there can be only one authority and one king; the authority of Heaven and its king, King Jesus. The Christian believer is part of the Heavenly Kingdom of God and his king is King Jesus. Islam is trying to change the earth into the likeness of its king, Allah. It is trying to usurp the King of Kings, Jesus, and bring about its authoritative government of demonic rules to all mankind. Christian believers must stand firm in true and faithful understanding of who they are and use their authority to stop both Islam and Allah.

The "Ecclesia" of God can and must take its rightful place in the earth as God's true representatives!

EPILOGUE

On May 1st, 2011, President Barack Obama announced the death of the planner and instigator of many killings in the name of Allah. Osama bin Laden, the mastermind of the World Trade attack, had been killed by United States military forces in Pakistan after being traced to a compound adjacent to what is equivalent to the U.S.A. West Point military academy. Bin Laden had been hiding in plain sight.

Many people throughout the world rejoiced at the news of bin Laden's death. The United States witnessed people around the White House, New York City and Ground Zero of the destroyed World Trade Center Twin Towers, and cities in general celebrating the death of a mass murderer. To some, it meant an end to a long nightmare of losing loved ones to a religious mindset that hates anything or anyone who differs.

It should be noted, however, that bin Laden, his henchmen, and al-Qaeda,[1] the Muslim extremists, who

---

[1] from Arabic *al-qa`ida* the base. A loosely-knit militant Islamic organization led and funded by Osama bin Laden, by whom it was established in the late 1980s from Arab volunteers who had fought the Soviet troops previously based in Afghanistan, known or believed to be behind a number of operations against Western, especially U.S.,

185

carried out the death of thousands, killed more Muslims than they did non-Muslims. Many in the Muslim communities throughout the world welcomed the death of bin Laden.

Bin Laden's death even started a conversation throughout many political arenas about the possibility of pulling all American military personnel from Afghanistan and other Middle East countries.

It seems that we non-Islamic-thinking people have forgotten or are just plain dull to the reality of motives of men like bin Laden. Bin Laden and Muslim extremists aren't out to kill non-Muslims because we have a different culture or live in democracy styled nations, they want to completely change who we claim as our God.

The base cause of the World Trade successful attack was supposedly because the United States foreign policy throughout the Middle East over the years had enraged so many Muslims that bin Laden and others like him had had enough and decided to bring Jihad to America.

This author believes that bin Laden's death will change nothing as far as Islamic thinking goes. Islam and its main tenet of world subjugation to Islam and Allah have

interests, including bomb attacks on two U.S. embassies in Africa in 1998 and the destruction of the World Trade Center in New York in 2001

not changed and there are those in authority in other countries who believe it is their duty to make that a reality.

Peace does not seem to be a motivating factor in the Koran. Agitation and war stand out as two things that promote Islam and submission to Allah. This premise is reinforced by the constant state of affairs in most Middle East nations that make Islam the religion and law of the land.

That mindset seems to be engrained in those who follow strict Islamic thinking. Even in the United States, and cities like Detroit, which has the largest Muslim population within the country, are having to address those who desire Sharia law opposed to the Constitution of the United States. Detroit and other large Muslim-impacted cities are seeing the agitated and warlike mentality coming to the forefront of political and social change.

How the Christian community responds to the mindset of Islamic thinking can make a difference, if we live our truths. Many Muslims have been won to the saving knowledge of Jesus. The one overriding factor to those Muslims who converted to Christianity was the love and support they witnessed towards them. Walls of hate and misunderstanding began to fall when the Christian community lived the truths they supposedly believed in. In other words, the word of God believed, lived out, and dispensed to others caused the Muslim neighbor to search for the truth in Christian scripture. A loving, scripture-dispensing, and understanding child of the true God can really make a difference!

APPENDIX A

END TIMES

I tread softly as I write this Appendix. But, I believe, in light of the events of history in the twentieth and twenty-first centuries, I can adequately give enough historical information and Scripture that would satisfy an honest searcher.

Probably one of the best informative teachings about the end-times comes from Ellis Skolfield and his books that teach and warn the world of the Islamic dangers to come. [1]

Many Christian teachers throughout modern times have held onto, I believe, a misinterpreted view of Scripture trying to prove the events in the book of Revelation. Their dogged belief that the anti-Christ would be the Catholic Pope and his one world government that would affect the whole world is silly at best. Also, it is comical to this student to think that Christians would be whisked away from the earth before any harm would come.

---

[1] Ellis Skolfield (Fort Myers, FL: Fish House Publishing), www.fishhousemininstries.com.

Why would God want to take out of the earth the very people who would proclaim the truth of His word?

My studies have proven to me that God has told us what He will do. He has given us the proper prophets to proclaim His intentions, and He has given the earth the witness of the Jew to prove who, how, and when He will bring about the end. The Old and the New Testaments are filled with timeline insights and prophetic warning, which have been correct even down to the very year.

Much of the end-time events, which were prophesied by Daniel, have come to pass. Daniel looked into the future under the anointing of the Spirit of God, and John looked back and forward in time under that same Spirit. Daniel spoke of Israel, the temple mount, the dispersing of the Jews throughout the world and their return to their promised home land, the total control of Jerusalem, and Israel being surrounded by Gentile nations. John's revelations will be fulfilled in the years ahead.

Daniel's and John's prophecies:

- *The 1290 days of Daniel 12:11, fulfilled in 688 AD by the construction of the Islamic Dome of the Rock.*
- *The 42 months of Revelation 11:2, fulfilled in 1967 AD by the freeing of Jerusalem from the Gentile control.*

- *The 1260 Days of Revelation 11:3, fulfilled in 1948 AD by the Jewish people returning to their homeland.*
- *The 1260 Days of Revelation 12:5, fulfilled in 1948 AD by the establishment of the new nation of Israel.*
- *The Time, Times and Half Time of Daniel 7:25, fulfilled in 1948 AD by the new nation of Israel.*
- *The Time, Times and Half Time of Daniel 12:7, fulfilled in 1967 AD by the freeing of Jerusalem.*
- *The Season and Time of Daniel 7:12, fulfilled in 1948 AD when Gentiles lost control of the Holy Land.* [2]

We can see from Scripture that the Abomination of Desolation (the Dome of the Rock), which is a building and not a person, completely fulfilled the prophecy of Daniel 12:11. This is important because it gives us a timeline to follow for the rest of the prophecies mentioned in Daniel and Revelation.

I strongly suggest the book *Islam In The End Times – The Religious Battle Behind The Headlines* by Ellis Skolfield for any honest searcher of end-time truth.[3] I also

---

[2] Ellis Skolfield, *Islam In The End Times – The Religious Battle Behind The Headlines* (Fort Myers, FL: Fish House Publishing, 2007), 79.

[3] Ibid.

suggest the book *The Islamic AntiChrist* by Joel Richardson.[4] Richardson's book focuses on the Muslim's belief in their end-time messiah, the Mahdi and other Islamic personalities. Although these two books speak of the end-times, they come from two different directions to inform of the "tribulation period," or the end-times. Also, I believe they are informers with a piece of the puzzle, if you will, but when taken as a whole, we can rightly realize the events that will soon happen in the Middle East and the world at large.

Islam

There are those within Islam who strongly believe in an end-time scenario whereby Islam will be the only religion on the planet and Allah will be worshipped. The adherents to this belief are not just a few fanatical Muslim believers, nor are they without influence in the Islamic world; Men like President Mahmoud Ahadinejad of Iran are believers in an Islamic end time.

President Mahmoud Ahmadinejad surprised not only many Westerners but also many Iranians when, during his first speech at the United Nations in 2005, he prayed for the hasty return of the Hidden Imam, the Mahdi, Shi'i

---

[4] Joel Richardson, *The Islamic AnitChrist* (Los Angeles, CA: WorldNetDaily, 2009).

Islam's messianic figure. When he greeted the world's Christians for the coming new year, he said he expects both Jesus and the Islamic Shiite messianic figure, Imam Mahdi, to return and "wipe away oppression."[5]

> I wish all the Christians a very happy new year and I wish to ask them a question as well, said Ahmadinejad, according to an Iranian Student News Agency report cited by YnetNews.com
>
> My one question from the Christians is: What would Jesus do if he were present in the world today? What would he do before some of the oppressive powers of the world who are in fact residing in Christian countries? Which powers would he revive and which of them would he destroy?
>
> If Jesus were present today, who would be facing him and who would be following him?[6]

When the Mahdi returns, the Muslims believe he will reign on earth for seven years before bringing about a final judgment and the end of the world.

---

[5] Robert Spencer, "Ahmadinejad, at UN, calls for the coming of the Mahdi" http://www.jihadwatch.org/2006/09/ahmadinejad-at-un-calls-for-the-coming-of-the-mahdi.html (accessed Jan. 2, 2011).

[6] Imam Mahdi, believed by Shiites to have disappeared as a child in 941 AD.

"All I want to say is that the age of hardship, threat and spite will come to an end someday and, God willing, Jesus would return to the world along with the emergence of the descendant of the Islam's holy prophet, Imam Mahdi, and wipe away every tinge of oppression, pain and agony from the face of the world," Ahmadinejad said.

"I emphatically declare that today's world, more than ever before, longs for just and righteous people with love for all humanity; and above all longs for the perfect righteous human being and the real savior who has been promised to all peoples and who will establish justice, peace and brotherhood on the planet," Ahmadinejad said. "Oh, Almighty God, all men and women are your creatures and you have ordained their guidance and salvation. Bestow upon humanity that thirsts for justice, the perfect human being promised to all by you, and make us among his followers and among those who strive for his return and his cause."[7]

Ahmadinejad is on record as stating he believes he is to have a personal role in ushering in the age of the Mahdi. In a November. 16, 2005, speech in Tehran, he said he sees

[7] Robert Spencer, "Ahmadinejad, at UN, calls for the coming of the Mahdi" http://www.jihadwatch.org/2006/09/ahmadinejad-at-un-calls-for-the-coming-of-the-mahdi.html (accessed Jan. 2, 2011).

his main mission in life as to *"pave the path for the glorious reappearance of Imam Mahdi, and may Allah hasten his reappearance."*[8]

Who is the Mahdi?

- The Mahdi will be a descendant of Muhammad of the line of Fatimah. He will be descended by one side (by one of the parents) by Hassan and by another by Hussain.
- He will have the same name as Muhammad.
- He will be a forerunner to Jesus' Islamic Rule.
- His coming will be accompanied by the raising of a Black Standard.
- His coming will be accompanied by the appearance of the Antichrist.
- There will be a lunar and solar eclipse within the same month of Ramadan.
- A star with a luminous tail will rise from the East before the coming of the Mahdi.
- He will establish the Caliphate.[9]
- He will fill the world with justice and fairness at a time when the world will be filled with oppression.

---

[8] Imam Mahdi, believed by Shiites to have disappeared as a child in 941 AD.

[9] The term **caliphate** "dominion of a caliph ('successor,')," (from the Arabic خلافة or khilāfa, Turkish: *Halife*) refers to the first system of government established in Islam, and represented the political unity of the Muslim Ummah (nation).

- He will have a broad forehead, a prominent nose, and a natural mascara will ring his eyes.
- His face shall shine upon the surface of the Moon.
- The name of the Mahdi's representative will begin with the first-letter of a prophet's name and a verse of the Koran: ک (English: *Y*).

We can see there is a strong belief in a coming savior in the mind of the average Muslim. Like the Christian, the Muslim is looking for someone to come and make the earth and all of its social, political, and personal problems go away. It is important to keep in mind that the Mahdi is a forerunner to the Muslim Jesus who they believe will come and correct the Jews and Christians. This Muslim Jesus is a second and most important personage in Islam.

Muslims do not believe that the Jesus of Christian Scripture died, but that He was saved from death by God, who took Him to heaven until He was to return to Earth and finish His ministry. This Jesus, Muslims believe, will return to Earth as a great prophet and a follower of the Mahdi and a most faithful Muslim.

The Muslim Jesus:

- Will become the overseer of the institutions and legal

enforcement of the Islamic *shariah* law.

Jesus, the son of Mary (this is not the Jesus of the Christian bible) will descend and will lead them judging amongst them according to the holy Qur'an and the Sunnah of the Prophet Muhammad.[10]

- Will be the great Islamic evangelist to further the truth of Islam and to correct the misrepresentations made by Christians and Jews.

Jesus will descend from heaven and espouse the cause of the Mahdi. The Christians and the Jews will see him abandon their faith in his godhead.[11]

- Will abolish Christianity.

The Prophet said: There is no prophet between me and him, this is, Jesus. He will descend to the earth...He will break the cross, kill swine, and abolish jizyah.

---

[10] Sideeque Veliankode, *Doomsday Portents and Prophecies* (Scarborough, Canada, 1999), 351.

[11] Muhammad Baqir Al-Sadr, and Murtada Mutahhari, *The Awaited Savior* (Karachi: Islamic Seminary Publications) prologue, 3.

Allah will perish all religions except Islam.[12]

- Will slay all Jews.

His [the Dajjals] followers the Yahudis [Jews], will number seventy thousand...Then Hadrat :Isa [Honorable Jesus] kills the Dajjal at the Gate of Hudd, near an Israeli airport, in the vailly of "Ifiq." The final war between the yahudis will ensue, and the Muslims will be victorious.[13]

- Will remain on earth for forty years, marry, have children and then die.

The Prophet said: There is no prophet between me and him, that is, Jesus... He will destroy the Antichrist and will live on the earth forty years and then he will die. The Muslims will pray over him.[14]

---

[12] Sunna Abu Dawud, Book 37, Number 4310, narrated by Abu Hurayrah. See also Sahih Bukhari, Volume 3, Book 43, Number 656.

[13] Mohammed Ali Ibn Zubair Ali, *Signs of Qiyama*, Translated by M. Afzal Hoosein Elias. (New Delhi: Abudul Naeem, 2004, http://members.cox.net/arshad/qiyaama.html (accessed February 2, 2010).

[14] Sunna Abu Dawud, Book 37, Number 4310, narrated by Abu Hurayrah.

The Muslims believe that the Jesus Christians believe in is really the *Dajjal* or false Jesus. A well-known Muslim apologist, Osamah Abdallah, believes and teaches the following:

> *Briefly, Christians believe that Jesus will come down to earth and fight for the state of Israel.... What seems to be quite ironic to me is that those Jews that Jesus is supposedly going to fight for don't even believe in Jesus as God himself nor as a Messenger of God.... Jesus never liked the Jews.... Now without being biased, we Muslims have a story that makes a lot more sense and is empty of contradictions! We believe that Jesus will come down to earth toward the end of the world time to fight the army of Satan which will be mostly from the "bad" Jews or "Zionist Jews" as we call them today, and the deceived from the Polytheist Christians or the Trinitarian Christians and the Pagan Polytheists such as Hindu, Buddhist, etc.... Some Jews and many Christians will be among the good and blessed who will fight with Jesus' side. The army of Satan will be led by a person who will claim to be Jesus Christ himself. The Muslims will call him the Dajjal or the Deceiver. The real Jesus' army will fight the Dajjal's army and defeat him. The empire of*

Israel will fall, and the religion of Islam will prevail. [15]

The belief of Abdallah and other Muslims who believe this description of these two Jesuses is amazing in light of the Hebraic/Christian Scripture that had come before the Koran. The Muslims and the Koran completely overlook or deny the Holy Scriptures that speak of Jesus and His life on the earth. But this would probably be the case if one would deny that the Jew has a right to exist and that Jesus of Nazareth was God and Man, that He died for all mankind, and that He was resurrected again.

Christianity

Christianity teaches, in the book of Revelation, that there will come upon the earth a time of great trouble, such as the world has never known before. This time is known as the Tribulation Period and Great Tribulation Period. It is the time that God will bring about His judgment upon the earth and cleanse the universe and mankind of all sin. There are different opinions by different scholars about the exact timing of the events mentioned in Revelation about

---

[15] Osamah Abdallah, *Islam: The True Religion of God Almighty,* http://www.answering-christianity.com/que5.htm (accessed Feb. 2, 2011).

the Tribulation/Great Tribulation period.[16] As a whole, however, the characters which populate the narrative in Revelation can pretty well be established. If one studies the Christian Scripture and the Koran, Hadits, and other Muslim commentaries, one can see the overwhelming similarities.

Most Christians believe in an end-time and usually accept the most popular teachings that God's wrath will be poured out as taught in Revelation. However, there are four ways to look at the timing of God's wrath and when the Church (Christians) would be taken off of this earth and into heaven by means of the rapture.[17] Those ways are Pre-tribulation Rapture, Mid-tribulation Rapture, Post-tribulation Rapture, and the one this student believes, the Pre-wrath Rapture.[18]

It is during the Tribulation/Great Tribulation period that the personage of the Antichrist and his False Prophet will come onto the scene of history, and then Jesus will

[16] This timing of the Tribulation/Great Tribulation is believed by most people to be seven years.

[17] The **Rapture** is a futurist interpretation of Christian eschatology, in which it is posited that Christians will be gathered together in the air to meet Christ at, or up to seven years prior to, his return.

[18] Marvin Rosenthal, *The Pre-Wrath Rapture of the Church* (Nashville, TN: Thomas Nelson, Inc., 1990).

return to Earth to receive the Christians in the air with Him and to bring God's judgment.

The Tribulation/Great Tribulation period will not come about until there is a world wide resurgence of nations and national thought to once and for all destroy Israel. Without going into an exhaustive study of the book of Revelation, both Old and New Testament Scripture, and scholars who have their own theories, I will just state some facts as I see them from Scripture about the end-time. I see in Scripture that Israel will be surrounded by nations who hate their very existence. I believe those nations are all Muslim nations that believe Allah is the only true god, that Muhammad is the final prophet from God, and that any religion other than Islam does not have the right to exist. Scripture mentions the ancient names of people who populated certain areas around Israel and in time became modern nations; Magog: (made up of Azerbaijan, Afghanistan, Turkestan, Chechnya, Turkey, Iran and Dagestan *(probably Syria)*, Meshech & Tubal *(modern Turkey)*, Persia *(Iran)*, Cush *(Sudan)*, Put *(Libya)*, Gomer *(Cappadocia)*, Togarmah *(Turkey again)*. All of these nations are Muslim and hate the Jew and will do anything to eliminate them as well as any other religion.

I see the revived empire that John [19] prophesied about to be the Turkish empire (Islamic) that defeated the Roman empire.[20] The Turkish empire was the seat of the Islamic caliphate, which was not abolished until 1923. Even today, Muslims look for the restoration of that caliphate,[21] and there has been talk of Turkey being its headquarters.

THE SPIRIT BEHIND THE HATE

The sin of mankind and the total disregard for God and His ways is what makes God pour out His wrath in the end times. I have mentioned the sin of Adam and the necessity of God bringing into the world Adam's offspring who would take that sin and bring redemption to mankind. Jesus was the perfect offspring of Adam who made it possible for all humans to know the true God. Mankind,

---

[19] Revelation 17:9-11.

[20] The Roman empire wasn't completely destroyed until 1453 AD by the Turks. The Turkish/Ottoman empire succeeded the Roman empire and ruled over the entire Middle East, including Jerusalem, for nearly five hundred years. The Turkish empire existed right up until 1909.

[21] The term **caliphate** "dominion of a caliph ('successor,')," (from the Arabic خلافة or khilāfa, Turkish: *Halife*) refers to the first system of government established in Islam and represented the political unity of the Muslim Ummah (nation).

however, has disregarded God's loving patience during the centuries of time and has continually listened to the same spirit that was in the Garden of Eden who tempted Adam. That spirit has been alive trying to dissuade mankind from believing in Adam's offspring, Jesus, who would be the sacrifice for Adam's rebellion. That spirit is called deceiver, liar, Satan, great serpent, and since Jesus came on the scene, the Antichrist.

The spirit of Antichrist has done everything possible to confuse, destroy, and murder the truth found in Holy Scripture and anyone who believes that message. The Antichrist spirit hates the Jews and Christians and promotes and propagates an ongoing lie to keep millions of people in ignorance to the truth. That spirit will do anything to attack Jesus because Jesus is the fulfillment of God's plan to save mankind. The major lies of the Antichrist spirit is *that Jesus is not the Christ/Messiah and savior of Israel and the world, that there is not a Father, Son (Jesus) and Holy Spirit, and that Jesus has not come in the flesh or God became man.*

> *But every spirit that does not acknowledge Jesus is not from God. This is the spirit of the antichrist, which you have heard is coming and even now is already in the world.*
>
> 1 John 4:3

*Who is the liar? It is the man who denies
that Jesus is the Christ. Such a man is the
antichrist – he denies the Father and the
Son. No one who denies the Son has the
Father; whoever acknowledges the Son has
the Father also.*

John 3:22-23

*Many deceivers, who do not acknowledge
Jesus Christ as coming in the flesh, have
gone out into the world. Any such person is
the deceiver and the antichrist.*

2 John 1:7

It is that same Antichrist spirit we see in Islam; the Koran
denies that Jesus is the Christ; it denies that God has a son,
the tri-unity of God, and the cross of Christ.[22] Allah,
Islam's god, as proved in the Koran, fulfills the Prophet
Daniel's revelation;[23] Allah speaks unheard of things
against the God of gods; he speaks against the Most High
and oppresses the saints (Christian and Jews) through the
Muslims.

One of the great hatreds we see the spirit of
Antichrist spouting in modern times is the hatred towards
the Jews. Islam does not hide its hatred for the Jew; the

---

[22] Surah 5:17, 10:68, 19:88-92, 9:30, 5:73 and 4:157-158.

[23] Daniel 7:25 and 11:36.

205

Koran, the Hadits, and most commentaries about the Jews are filled with hatred for God's chosen people. It can't be denied that Islam and Muslims are the single most anti-Semitic[24] force against Israel and the Jews.

THE ANTICHRIST GOAL

The main goal of the Antichrist is to dominate the world and to be worshipped in the place of God.

> *He (beast) was given power to make war against the saints and to conquer them. And he was given authority over every tribe, people, language and nation. All inhabitants of the earth will worship the beast – all whose names have not been written in the book of life belonging to the Lamb that was slain from the creation of the world.*
>
> Revelation 13: 7-8.

WHO IS THE BEAST?

We know from Scripture that the spirit of Antichrist is none other than Satan himself. He is the one who is pulling the strings of men, nations and empires to hate God's people, both Jew and Christian, but his main aim is

---

[24] Semitic: In linguistics and ethnology, **Semitic** (from the Biblical "Shem," Hebrew: שם, translated as "name", Arabic: سَامِيّ) was first used to refer to a language family of largely Middle Eastern origin, now called the **Semitic languages.** This family includes the ancient and modern forms of Akkadian, Amharic, Arabic, Aramaic, Ge'ez, Hebrew, Maltese, Phoenician, Tigre and Tigrinya among others. The term "anti-Semitic" (or "anti-Semite") overwhelmingly refers to Jews only.

to be worshipped instead of God. Satan uses anyone he deems weak and will not honor the true God. He uses empires, both in the past, present and future. The beast we see in Revelation represents empires that once were and are now revived. Revelation 13:1-2 tells us what the beast looked like. It is important to keep in mind that most of the imagery is speaking about empires that once ruled the known world.

> *And I stood upon the sand of the sea, and saw a beast rise up out of the sea* (sea represents peoples of the earth), *having seven heads and ten horns* (rulers and their kingdoms), *and upon his horns ten crowns (rulers), and upon his heads the name of blasphemy* (the motto or attitudes the rulers proclaimed against God). *And the beast which I saw was like unto a leopard* (Greek empire), *and its feet were as the feet of a bear* (Medo-Persian empire), *and his mouth as the mouth of a lion* (Babylonian empire): *and the dragon gave him his power, and his seat, and great authority* (Parenthetical comments mine).

The offspring of the ancient three empires of the Greece, Medo-Persian, and Babylonian empires today are Iraq, Iran, and Syria-Lebanon. These nations today are all Muslim and hate the Jew and anyone who denies that Allah is God and that Muhammad is his prophet. This is

207

important because we must understand that Satan's (the Dragon) plan, tactics, and wordings have not changed, and he will war against all those who live upon the earth to gain worship. Islam is of the spirit of Antichrist, which the earth is now and will have to deal with in the future.

Joel Richardson in his book, *The Islamic AntiChrist,* chronicles what he believes the Islamic antichrist, as seen in the Koran, Hadits and other Muslim writings, and Jesus, as seen in the Bible, have in common and their similarities. I log them here in part and with minor changes:[25]

- Bible: The Antichrist is an unparalleled political military and religious leader that will emerge in the last days.

  o Islam: The Mahdi is an unparalleled political, military, and religious leader that will emerge in the last days.

- Bible; The False Prophet is a secondary prominent figure that will emerge in the last days who will support the Antichrist.

  o Islam: The Muslim Jesus is a secondary prominent figure that will emerge in the last days to support the Mahdi.

---

[25] Richardson, Joel, *The Islamic AntiChrist* (New York, NY: WND Books, 2009), 171-175.

- Bible: The Antichrist and the False Prophet together will have a powerful army that will do great damage to the earth in an effort to subdue every nation and dominate the world.

  o Islam: The Mahdi and the Muslim Jesus will have a powerful army that will attempt to control every nation on the earth and dominate the world.

- Bible: The False Prophet is described essentially as a dragon in lamb's clothing.

  o Islam: The Muslim Jesus comes bearing the name of the one that the world knows as "the Lamb of god," Jesus Christ. Yet the Muslim Jesus comes to murder all those who do not submit to Islam.

- Bible: The Antichrist and the False Prophet establish a new world order.

  o Islam: The Mahdi and the Muslim Jesus establish a new world order.

- Bible: The Antichrist and the False Prophet institute new laws for the whole earth.

  o Islam: The Mahdi and the Muslim Jesus institute Islamic law all over the earth.

- Bible: The Antichrist is said to "change the times."

  o Islam: It is quite certain that if the Mahdi established Islam all over the earth, he would discontinue the use of Saturday and Sunday as the weekend or day of rest, changing to Friday, the holy day of Islam. Also, he would most certainly eliminate the Gregorian calendar and replace it with the Islamic calendar currently used in every Islamic country.

- Bible: The Antichrist and the False Prophet will both be powerful religious leaders who will attempt to institute a universal world religion.

  o Islam: The Mahdi and the Muslim Jesus will institute Islam as the only religion on the earth.

- Bible: The Antichrist and the False Prophet will execute anyone who does not submit to their world religion. They will use beheading.

  o Islam: Likewise, the Mahdi and the Muslim Jesus will execute anyone who does not submit to Islam. They will use beheading.

- Bible: The Antichrist and the False Prophet will attack to conquer and seize Jerusalem.

- o Islam: The Mahdi and the Muslim
  Jesus will attack to re-conquer and
  seize Jerusalem for Islam.

- Bible: The False Prophet is said to do
  many miracles to deceive as many as
  possible into supporting the Antichrist.

  - o Islam: The Mahdi is said to control
    the weather and the crops. His face is
    said to glow. We can also assume
    that since Jesus is viewed as having
    been empowered by Allah to work
    miracles when He was here on Earth
    the first time, He will most likely be
    expected to continue to do so when
    He returns.

- Bible: The Antichrist is described as
  riding on a white horse.

  - o Islam: The Mahdi is described as
    riding on a white horse.

- Bible: The Antichrist is said to make a
  peace treaty with Israel for seven years.

  - o Islam: The Mahdi is said to make a
    peace treaty through a Jew for
    exactly seven years.

- Bible: Jesus, the Jewish Messiah, will
  return to defend the Jews in Israel from
  military attack from a vast coalition of

nations led by the Antichrist and the False Prophet.

o Islam: The Dajjal, the Islam Antichrist, will gain a great Jewish following and claim to be Jesus Christ; he will fight against the Mahdi and the Muslim Jesus.

- Bible: The spirit of Antichrist specifically denies the most unique and central doctrines of Christianity, namely the Tri-unity, the incarnation, and the substitutionary death of Jesus on the Cross.

o Islam: Islam, doctrinally and spiritually, specifically denies the most unique and central doctrines of Christianity, namely the Tri-unity, the incarnation, and the substitutionary death of Jesus on the Cross.

I have mentioned all of the above about the end times and the characters in the soon coming events on Earth because of the overwhelming written and historical proof from my own and shared research. Islam, Judaism and Christianity are on a collision course that will end in God pouring His wrath out upon the earth and to save all those who trust in Him. Every human needs to know these things!

My research has led me to believe that we must be careful in putting time tables to the end time. I see much of what Daniel and Ezekiel prophesied about as already having taken place. I do see, however, that in the end time there will be an Antichrist, False Prophet, and other individuals who will deceive the earth and try to prevent God from saving mankind. I see a religious system that is now in place and will soon become more united in their goal of world domination. I see Islam as that religious and political system.

WHAT'S GOING ON NOW?

Toward the end of 2010 the earth began to see much upheaval in the Muslim nations. After the fall in Iraq of its leader Saddam Hussein, there was an upsurge of Islamic terrorism around the world. Other Islamic believers saw the open door in Iraq to promote the Islamic agenda and its laws. Those Islamic insurgents believe that no foreign government, army or political system should be on Muslim soil. It is an affront to what Islam teaches and strongly wars against.

At the beginning of 2011, many other Islamic nations are in turmoil as the citizens of their countries protest against government control that denies human rights and social justice. These nations are seeing a cry for

213

freedom as they observe it in the Western nations. Those Western nations, however, are based upon a Judeo-Christian system of beliefs and totally deny any rabid belief in a one religion society. For that reason, I believe, the quest for freedom the citizens in the turmoiled countries seek will elude them, and in its place will come an Islamic controlled group of nations, which will in the end bring about the lost *caliphate* Islam dreams of.

Throughout the world today, year 2011, Islam is ever increasing and becoming a threat to many societies. Soon many countries will have over 50% Muslim population. As of October 7, 2009, the following nations were made up of 50% or more Muslims (According to thePew Research Center.) [26]

Africa	Middle East	Asia-Pacific
Mauritania - 99.1%		Turkey – 98%
Mali – 92.5%	Palestinian territories – 98%	Azerbaijan – 99.2%
Niger – 98.6%		Kazakhstan – 56.4%
Nigeria – 50.4%	Lebanon – 59.3%	Uzbekistan – 96.3%
Chad – 55.8%	Jordan - 98.2%	Turkmenistan – 93.1%
Burkina Faso 59%	Syria – 92.2%	Kyrgyzstan – 86.3%
Guinea – 84.4%	Iraq – 99%	
Senegal – 96.0%		
Gambia – 95%		

[26]Pew Research Center "Mapping the Global Muslim Population," The Pew Forum on Religion & Public Life, http://pewforum.org/Muslim/Mapping-the-Global-Muslim-Population.aspx (accessed Feb. 10, 2010).

Sierra Leone – 71.3%	Kuwait – 95%	Tajikistan – 84.1%
Djibouti – 96.9%	Saudi Arabia – 97%	Afghanistan – 99.7%
Somalia – 98.5%	Bahrain – 81.2%	Pakistan – 96.3%
Comoros – 98.3%	Qatar – 77.5%	Bangladesh – 89.6%
Mayotte – 98.4%	United Arab Emirates – 76.2%	Malaysia – 60.4%
Western Sahara – 99.4%	Oman – 87.7%	Maldives – 98.4%
Morocco – 99%	Yemen – 99.1%	Brunei – 67.2%
Algeria – 98%		Indonesia – 88.2%
Tunisia – 99.5%		
Libya – 96.6		
Egypt – 94.6		
Sudan – 71.3%		
Somalia – 98.5%		

In the countries that have over fifty percent Muslims, their influence is solidly entrenched and the government is made up of mostly Muslim officials, and their system of government usually is in part, if not all, influenced by Sharia law. In countries that have less than five percent Muslims, there usually is not much of an effect on the population. But, as soon as the population of Muslims become greater than five percent, they seem to have an inordinate influence in the society. The countries of France, Philippines, Sweden, Switzerland, The Netherlands, and Trinidad & Tobago are seeing an attempt by the Muslim population to rule themselves within their ghettos by the Islamic law, Sharia. [27] In countries such as

---

[27] Sharia (Arabic: شريعة *šarīah*, IPA: [ʃaˈriːʕa], "way" or "path") is the sacred law of Islam. Most Muslims believe Sharia is

Guyana, India, Israel, Kenya and Russia, which have from ten to fifteen percent of Muslims, we see a lawless attitude toward their government, and violence is common, which is promoted by the Muslims. Those nations that have from twenty to fifty percent Muslims are seeing rioting, jihad type formations and even widespread massacres of other ethnic and religious peoples. The countries of Ethiopia and Bosnia, are such countries. And when a nation becomes more than fifty percent Muslim there is no stopping persecution of non-Islamic believers. In those countries that are predominantly Muslim, the government and social norms of the society are controlled by Islamic thinking and the schools all become Madrasses; the normal reading, writing and arithmetic is taught, but the Koran is the only word and basically the only text book adhered to. [28]

---

derived from two primary sources of Islamic law: the divine revelations set forth in the Qur'an, and the example set by the Islamic Prophet Muhammad in the Sunnah.

[28] A typical Islamic school usually offers two courses of study: a *hifz* course teaching memorization of the Qur'an (the person who commits the entire Qur'an to memory is called a hafiz); and an 'alim course leading the candidate to become an accepted scholar in the community. A regular curriculum includes courses in Arabic, tafsir (Qur'anic interpretation), sharī'ah (Islamic law), hadiths (recorded sayings and deeds of Prophet Muhammad), mantiq (logic), and Muslim history.

This increase of the Islamic population in the world and its anti-Christian and anti-Jewish stance seems to be the very danger that the book of Revelation warns mankind of. Since 1948, the twenty-one Arab countries have suffered 30 wars, 63 successful revolutions, at least 75 unsuccessful revolutions, and the murder of 36 heads of state.[29]

---

[29] Peter Hammond, *Slavery, Terrorism and Islam – The Historical Roots and Contemporary Threat (USA: Xulonpress)*,39.

APPENDIX B

THE CRUSADES

The politically-correct thinking about the Crusades has been to see the European crusaders as an offensive force of murderers that raped, pillaged and destroyed their way to and in the Holy Lands. This myth has been propagated for centuries and is always used by those who either don't understand Islam or refuse to believe that

> *The crusaders were a defensive force to protect the Holy Land!*

there were other reasons for the Crusades as a whole. In reality, the crusaders were a defensive force trying to protect the Holy Land and its people from those who would destroy Christian places and peoples.

Islam and its mind set of Jihad destroyed more than half of the Christian church worldwide from the seventh to the tenth century. The Muslims moved through Northern Africa, then into Spain, and throughout Asia Minor, and then into the Balkans. All of those areas were in no way a social or economical threat to Islam but were in its way of becoming the religion of the world. And into the tenth century, Muslims had either destroyed or relocated more than 50% of all Christians in the world at that time.

The mentality that drove Muslims into the Northern parts of Africa and then towards Europe was the idea of *"Dar-al"* (The House of...); one being *Dar-al-Islam* (the House of Islam) and the other *Dar-al-Harb* (the House of War). Any nation that was not submitting to Islam would be considered to be at war with Islam and its prophet because it was not under *Sharia Law.*

The idea that a nation was not at peace if it wasn't under Sharia Law is another form of warped thinking. Islam is an Arabic word that means submission, surrender or subjugation. A Muslim is one who submits, and the way Muslims submit is by finding peace through Islam. Therefore, Islam teaches and Muslims believe they are "peacemakers" and use arguments, wars, intrigue, threats, economics, terrorism, and any other means possible to induce Islam into a region, area or people.

> *And fight them until there is no more tumult or oppression, and there prevails justice and faith in Allah altogether and everywhere.*
> Surah 8:39

The European peoples and Christian governments had enough and finally on November 27, 1095 AD, the pope pleaded with the European knights of all realms to rescue the Holy Land from the Islamic menace. The knights did not consider themselves as conquerors, but only God's soldiers who were freeing the Holy Land from those who were destroying and desecrating it. Yes, the Crusaders did terrible things, and what they did was not in the spirit of Christianity and Christ likeness, but without the Jihad of Islam they would not have had to go in the first place.

When the Crusaders reached the walls of Jerusalem, they offered terms of surrender to the Muslims who quickly denied the terms with blasphemous cursings and urinating on icons and crucifixes of Christ. On July 15, 1099, during an eclipse of the sun, the Crusaders overtook the walls of the city and completely destroyed the Saracens who had desecrated the holy places.

The Muslims were able to retake the Holy Land on September 17, 1187, by the famous Saladin. King Richard the Lionhearted of England, Emperor Frederick Barbarossa of Germany, and King Phillip of France were the leaders of the Third Crusade who won battles off and on, but after the death of Saladin Jerusalem once again was conquered by the Muslims in 1229 AD. By the end of the 13th century, the Crusaders who were left in the Holy Lands were defeated, and the Crusades were finished. The Holy Land was then in the hands of those who deny any other god but Allah.

It should never be forgotten that the Crusades started after five centuries of Muslim Jihad and the killing of hundreds of thousands of people who lived in what was known as a Christian world. Those peoples were forcibly converted, conquered or annihilated. The Crusaders wanted only to remove the Muslim invaders from the lands that had previously been Christian and restore freedom to the Holy Land and its places.

The Crusades ended over 700 years ago, but Muslim Jihad continues to this very day and threatens countries, peoples and religions that have not attacked or desire to attack Islam. It is quite possible that if the Crusades had never happened, Europe or America may not have existed as free continents as they are.

APPENDIX C

THE DESCENDANT OF ISHMAEL?

Much has been said about the Muslims' claims of Muhammad being a descendant of Ishmael. Their claim that Abraham's attempted sacrifice of his son Ishmael does not track in the Biblical account found in Genesis 22:2-11.

Then God said, "Take your son, your only son, Isaac, whom you love, and go to the region of Moriah. Sacrifice him there as a burnt offering on one of the mountains I will tell you about." Early the next morning Abraham got up and saddled his donkey. He took with him two of his servants and his son Isaac. When he had cut enough wood for the burnt offering, he set out for the place God had told him about. On the third day Abraham looked up and saw the place in the distance. He said to his servants, "Stay here with the donkey while I and the boy go over there. We will worship and then we will come back to you." Abraham took the wood for the burnt offering and placed it on his son Isaac, and he himself carried the fire and the knife. As the two of them went on together, Isaac spoke up and said to his father Abraham, "Father?" "Yes, my son?" Abraham replied. "The fire and wood are here," Isaac said, "but where is the lamb for the burnt offering?" Abraham answered,

223

"God himself will provide the lamb for the burnt offering, my son." And the two of them went on together. When they reached the place God had told him about, Abraham built an altar there and arranged the wood on it. He bound his son Isaac and laid him on the altar, on top of the wood. Then he reached out his hand and took the knife to slay his son. But the angel of the Lord called out to him from heaven, "Abraham! Abraham!" "Here I am," he replied. "Do not lay a hand on the boy," he said. "Do not do anything to him. Now I know that you fear God, because you have not withheld from me your son, your only son." Abraham looked up and there in a thicket he saw a ram caught by its horns. He went over and took the ram and sacrificed it as a burnt offering instead of his son. So Abraham called that place The Lord Will Provide. And to this day it is said, "On the mountain of the Lord it will be provided." The angel of the Lord called to Abraham from heaven a second time and said, "I swear by myself, declares the Lord, that because you have done this and have not withheld your son, your only son, I will surely bless you and make your descendants as numerous as the stars in the sky and as the sand on the seashore. Your descendants will take possession of the cities of their enemies, and through your offspring all nations on earth will be blessed, because you have obeyed me."

Gen 22:2-18

The Biblical account states very plainly that it was Isaac whom Abraham was going to sacrifice by God's command. To claim that it was Ishmael is changing Scripture to prove one's own story.

Ishmael and his mother Hagar moved to the Desert of Paran and later Ishmael's descendants occupied the Fertile Crescent region, an area about a thousand miles from Arabia. Scripture tells us just where Ishmael would live: *"and he shall dwell in the presence of all his brethren."* *Genesis 16:12.* He and his descendants lived between his brethren; his brethren were his half brother Isaac and his sons Jacob and Esau. Jacob lived in Canaan, also known as Palestine, and Esau lived in southern Jordan. Ishmael lived in between the two regions in the Desert of Paran and continually lived there. Scripture then tells us that Ishmael even died where he lived all his life;

> *Altogether, Ishmael lived a hundred and thirty-seven years. He breathed his last and died, and he was gathered to his people. His descendants settled in the area from Havilah to Shur, near the border of Egypt, as you go toward Asshur.*
>
> Gen 25:17-18.

Muhammad could not have been a descendant of Ishmael because he (Muhammad) was from the Sabaean Yemen family and Ishmael's linage became extinct many centuries before Muhammad's family left Yemen. Ishmael's people lived in the Fertile Crescent desert area.

Historians know that Muhammad's family lived in Saba-Yemen. In the fifth century AD, Qusayy Bin Kilab, the 8th ancestor of Muhammad, made an alliance of many Yemeni families forming Quraish, the tribe from which Muhammad later came. These families came to Mecca in the 5th century AD. The city of Mecca wasn't even built until the 4th century AD by the Khuzaa'h tribe. The Ishmaelites disappeared about 1,100 years before the family line of Muhammad. Muhammad's tribe could not have lived in the same locations as the Ishmaelite tribes at any time throughout history.

The misguided belief that Muhammad was a descendant of Ishmael came from the Muslim writer Ibn Ishak around 770-775 AD. Ishak wrote a false genealogy of Ishmael, which has stuck to this day. He said that Muhammad came from the tribe of Nabaioth. The Nabaioths, however, were a nomadic tribe who lived in the Sinai and Fertile Crescent deserts, but disappeared after the 7th century BC. History, archeology, and genealogy do not support the claims that Muhammad or Islam came from Ishmael.

Muhammad denied being a descendant of Ishmael, and rejected all genealogies of himself by others. Dr. Rafat Amari quotes Halabieh stating "Mohammad genealogized himself regarding his ancestors until he reached al-Nather bin Kinaneh, then he said, "Anyone who claimed otherwise or added further ancestors, has lied."[1]

---

[1] Dr. Rafat Amari, *Islam: In Light of History* (Prospect Heights, IL: Religion Research Institute, 2004), 334.

Rape victim, 13, stoned to death in Somalia

The above headline from the English news organization *Guardian News and Media Limited* and their web site www.guardian.co.uk reported on Sunday November 2, 2008 (<u>Chris McGreal</u>, Africa correspondent) that a 13-year old girl had been stoned for adultery after she reported being raped.

> *An Islamist rebel administration in Somalia had a 13-year-old girl stoned to death for adultery after the child's father reported that three men had raped her.*

> *Amnesty International said the al-Shabab militia, which controls the southern port city of Kismayo, arranged for a group of 50 men to stone Aisha Ibrahim Duhulow in front of a crowd of about 1,000 spectators.*

> *Duhulow's father told Amnesty that when they tried to report her rape to the militia, the child was accused of adultery and detained. None of the men Duhulow accused was arrested.*

The sad account of this poor innocent girl sheds light again, and confirms the ongoing terror Islam promotes amongst its own followers. Even when people in the crowd that day tried to save the raped victim they were thwarted from doing so, and even one young boy was killed.

This, all too often, account of Islam's attitude towards women brings into focus a major difference between Christianity and Islam. Christianity demands understanding, love, acceptance and forgiveness, but Islam demands a submission that no human can live up to, much less fall in line with a double standard of demands.

The men who raped the 13-year girl were never brought to justice and because she had no male witnesses to the rape, other than the rapists, she was considered an adulteress and worthy of death by stoning.

Compare this stoning in Somalia, and the biblical account of an adulteress women who actually was caught in the act, and we can see why Christianity speaks of love and Islam speaks just the opposite.

The teachers of the law and the Pharisees brought in a woman caught in adultery. They made her stand before the group and said to Jesus, "Teacher, this woman was caught in the act of adultery. In the Law Moses commanded us to stone such women. Now what do you say?" They were using this question as a trap, in order to have a basis for accusing him. But Jesus bent down and started to write on the ground with his finger. When they kept on questioning him, he straightened up and said to them, "If any one of you is without sin, let him be the first to throw a stone at her." Again he stooped down and wrote on the ground. At this, those who heard began to go away one at a time, the older ones first, until only Jesus was left, with the woman still standing there. 10 Jesus straightened up and asked her, "Woman, where are they? Has no one condemned you?" "No one, sir," she said. "Then neither do I condemn you," Jesus declared. "Go now and leave your life of sin."

John 8:3-11

GLOSSARY of Muslim Words

Allah - the god.

Burqa - A burqa is a head-to-toe covering worn exclusively by women. It is designed to conceal the entire body, including the face.

Caliphate - Dominion of a caliph (successor).

Dhimmi – "People of the Book"; Christians and Jews.

Hadith – Accepted accounts of what Muhammad said and did. Written by those who witnessed Muhammad and heard his words.

Hajji – The pilgrimage to Mecca.

Imam – Non-clerical leader of prayer in a mosque.

Intifada – Uprising.

Islam – Submission to the will of Allah.

Jihad – Holy War, struggle or striving.

Jinn - In Islam, jinns are fiery spirits (Qur'an 15:27) particularly associated with the desert. The highest of the jinns is Iblis, formerly called Azazel, the prince of darkness, or the Devil.

Kaaba – A cube-shaped structure in Mecca. Held many idols before Muhammad, but holds the Black Stone, which has been considered sacred for centuries.

233

Madrasa – An Islamic religious school.

Mahdi – The Imam Shi'i expected to return to Earth and bring perfect justice.

Minaret – A narrow tower attached to a mosque from which the call of prayer is announced for Muslims.

Monophsite – Belief that Christ was only divine, as opposed to being both human and divine.

Monotheists – Those who believe in one God.

Muslim – One who submits to Allah's will.

Qibla – The direction Muslims face (toward Mecca) when praying.

Koran (Qur'an) – Recite or recitation.

Ramadan – The ninth month of the Islamic lunar calendar in which Muslims fast from sunrise to sunset.

Rukhieh – Bewitching.

Salat – Prayer.

Shahadah – The Islamic confession of faith, "There is no god but God, and Muhammad is his prophet."

Sharia – Straight path; Islamic law.

Shirk – To deny that Allah is God.

Sunna – Tradition.

Sura or Surah – Chapter of the Koran.

Umma – Muslim community.

Zakat – Alms; fixed at the annual rate of 2.5 percent of a Muslim's net worth.

BIBLIOGRAPHY

Abdallah, Osamah. *Islam: The True Religion of God Almighty* http://www.answering-christianity.com.

Al-Sadr, Muhammad, Baqir, and Murtada Mutahhari. *The Awaited Savior* Karachi: Islamic Seminary Publications.

Alfano, Sean. *Grim Milestone for U.S. Soldiers Killed in Iraq, Afghanistan* CBS News Washington, Sept. 22, 2006, Available at http://www.cbsnews.com/stories/2006/09/22/terror/main2035427.shtml.

Amari, Rafat. *Islam: In Light of History*, Prospect Heights, IL: Religion Research Institute, 2004.

_____. *Occultism in the Family of Mohammed*, Religion Research Institute, 2004, http://religionresearchinstitute.org/Mohammad/occultism.htm.

Andrew, Brother. *For The Love Of My Brothers* Orange, CA: Bethany House Publishing, 1998.

Assaf, Bruce W. Behind *The Veil of Radical Islam – The Coming War* Belleville, Ontario, Canada: Guardian Books, 2007.

Bogle, Emory C. *Islam Origin & Belief* Austin, TX: University of Texas Press, 1998.

Bourg, Austin De. *Insights into the Mystery of the Trinity* Enumclaw, WA: WinePress Publishing, 2006.

Bauckham, Richard, et al. *Jesus 2000* Oxford, England: Lion Publishing plc, 1989.

Cowell, Alan. *Book Buried in Irish Bog Is Called a Major Find* The New York Times, July 27, 2006, Available at http://www.nytimes.com/2006/07/27/books/27psal. html

Crimp, Susan and Joel Richardson. *Why We Left – Former Muslims Speak Out* New York, NY: WND Books, Inc., 2008.

Donaldson, Catherine. *South Korea Confirms Hostage Killed* Fox News.com, June 23, 2004, Available at http://www.foxnews.com/story/0,2933,123343,00.ht ml.

Evans, Robert. *The Seven Messianic Festivals* Columbus, GA: Brentwood Christian Press, 2001.

Gabriel, Mark. *Jesus and Muhammad: Profound Differences and Surprising Similarities* Lake Mary, FL: Frontline, A Strange Company, 2004.

___. *The Unfinished Battle – Islam and the Jews* Lake Mary, FL: Frontline, A Strange Company, 2003.

Hammond, Peter. *Slavery, Terrorism and Islam – The Historical Roots and Contemporary Threat* USA: Xulon Press, 2000.

Jenkins, Philip. *Hidden Gospels: How the Search for Jesus Lost Its Way* New York: Oxford University Press, 2001.

Jones, Alan. *The Koran* Introduction, xx. London: Phoenix, a division of the Orion Publishing Group Ltd., 2001.

Karl-Heinz Ohlig and Gerd-R. Puin. *The Hidden Origins of Islam* Amherst, NY: Prometheus Books, 2010.

Keathley, J. Hampton. *The Tinity (Triunity) of God* Available at http://bible.org/article/trinity-triunity-god.

Lockyer, Herbert. *All The Messianic Prophecies Of The Bible* Grand Rapids, MI: Zondervan Publishing House, 1973.

M. Ali. *Islam Reviewed* Fort Myers, FL: Fish House Publishing, 1999.

Mikhail, Labib. *Is Allah of Muslims the God of Christians?* Available at http://www.thespiritofislam.com/god-allah/45-would-you-elaborate-on-that-very-first-point.html

McGreat, Chris. *Rape victim, 13, stoned to death in Somalia* Guardin.co.uk, 2 November 2008, Available at http://www.guardian.co.uk/world/2008/nov/02/somalia-gender.

Meelhuysen, Ed. *Dating Creation and Understanding the Jubilee Calendar* 1993-2008, Available at

http://www.bibleplus.org/creation/datingcreation.ht
m.

Murk, Jim. *Islam Rising - The Never Ending Jihad Against Christianity* Book One, Springfield, MO: 21st Century Press, 2006.

___. *Islam Rising - The Never Ending Jihad Against The Jew and Israel* Book Two, Springfield, MO: 21st Century Press, 2007.

Niles, Randall. *Dead Sea Scrolls – A Compelling Find, All About Archaeology* Available at http://www.allaboutarchaeology.org/dead-sea-scrolls.htm.

Pew Research Center *Mapping the Global Muslim Population*
The Pew Forum on Religion & Public Life, http://pewforum.org/Muslim/Mapping-the-Global-Muslim-Population.aspx.

Qutb, Sayyid. *The Right to Judge* Available at http://www.islamworld.net/docs/justice.html.

Richardson, Joel. *The Islamic AnitChrist* Los Angeles, CA: WorldNetDaily, 2009.

Robinson, B.A. *Growth Rate of Christianity & Islam* Religious Tolerance, Nov. 6, 2001 Available at http://www.religioustolerance.org/growth_isl_chr.ht
m.

Rosen, Ceil. *Christ in the Passover* Chicago, Il: Moody Press, 1978.

Rosenthal, Marvin. *The Pre-Wrath Rapture of the Church* Nashville, TN: Thomas Nelson, Inc., 1990.

Sahih al-Bukhari. *(the Correct books of Bukhar)*: English translation by Dr. Muhammad Mushasin Khan Available at http://www.usc.edu/schools/college/crcc/engageme nt/resources/texts/muslim/hadith/bukhari/009.sbt.ht ml.

Sanders, John. *The God Who Risks* Second Edition, Downers Grove, IL: IVP Academic, 2007.

Scrib.com. *Jesus in Every Book of the Bible* http://www.scribd.com/doc/40663295/Jesus-in-Every-Book-of-the-Bible (accessed February 8, 2011).

Skolfield, Ellis. *Islam In The End Times – The Religious Battle Behind The Headlines* Fort Myers, FL: Fish House Publishing, 2007.

Shoebat, Walid. *Why I Left Jihad – The Root of Terrorism and the Return of Radical Islam* USA: Top Executive Media, 2005.

Shoebat, Walid and Joel Richardson. *God's War on Terror* USA: Top Executive Media, 2008.

Spencer, Robert. *The Politically Incorrect Guide to Islam (and the Crusades)* Washington, DC, Regnery Publishing, Inc., 2005.

Stafford, Tim. *Knowing the Face of God – The Search for a Personal Relationship with God* Grand Rapids, MI: Zondervan Publishing House, 1986.

Stalinsky, Steven. *Dealing in Death, The Middle East Media Research* May 24, 2004, Available at http://old.nationalreview.com/comment/stalinsky20 0405240846.asp.

Veliankode, Sideeque M.A. *Doomsday Portents and Prophecies* Scarborough, Canada, 1999.

Warraq, Ibn. *Virgins? What Virgins? And Other Essays* Amherst, NY: Prometheus Books, 2010

Westmarck, Edward. *The Origin and Development of the Moral Ideas* London: MacMillan and Company, 1917.

Whiston, William A. M., The Works of Flavius Josephus, IV, Grand Rapids, MI: Baker Book House, 1979.

Zubair, Ali. *Mohammed Ali Ibn. Signs of Qiyama* Translated by M. Afzal Hoosein Elias. (New Delhi: Abudul Naeem, 2004, http://members.cox.net/arshad/qiyaama.html.

To order other books by Dr. Gwynn:
MEG Enterprises Publishers
PO Box 2165
Reidsville, GA 30453
Order on line at:
www.murlgwynn.com

www.ingramcontent.com/pod-product-compliance
Lightning Source LLC
Chambersburg PA
CBHW051818090426
42736CB00011B/1548